DARING TO BELIEVE

A Memoir of a Living Kidney Donor

AMY GRAY-CUNNINGHAM

DARING TO BELIEVE
Copyright © 2020 by Amy Gray-Cunningham

All rights reserved. Printed in the United States of America. No part of this book may be used or reproduced in any manner whatsoever without written permission except in the case of brief quotations embodied in critical articles or reviews.

For information contact :
amygraycunningham@gmail.com
www.amygraycunningham.com

Printed by CreateSpace, An Amazon.com Company

Book and Cover designed by Amy Gray-Cunningham
ISBN-10: 1985633914
ISBN-13: 978-1985633919

First Edition: March 2018
Second Edition: September 2020

Dedication

I dedicate this book to all the living kidney donors—past, present, and future. And to the families of the donors who experience this miracle with them.

And, to all those who have dared to believe in the impossible. Maybe you didn't donate a kidney, but perhaps God led you to build a school. Or, create a much-needed water supply in a foreign country. Or, build a homeless shelter. Or, take food to the elderly. Or, smile at the person next to you on the bus who thought about suicide but decided against it because you saw and acknowledged him.

Whatever you've been led to do, thank you for listening to your inner calling and daring to believe it was possible!

May your blessings be plentiful!

Acknowledgments

First, last, and always, I want to acknowledge and thank the Source of Everything—God. This journey we've been on has been incredible, and I look forward to experiencing many more miracles in this lifetime and possibly others. I will love You forever and always.

Second, my soul-mate, life partner, best friend, and lover—my devoted husband, Chuck Cunningham. Without you, I wouldn't be who I am today. You've been my greatest champion and supporter. You've kept me grounded, yet, given me wings when I needed to fly. Thank you for always believing in me. I will love you forever and always.

Next, my mother, Linda Price. You've taught me so much about faith, love, compassion, mercy, and forgiveness. You are everything I wanted to be and could hope to become. I believe that before I was born, God and I picked you for my mother. You are my earth angel—always there to help and support me. I will love you forever and always.

To Alex, my first-born—my beautiful son. You came into my life just when I needed you the most. The moment I looked into your angelic blue eyes, I couldn't imagine loving anyone as much as I loved you. You've grown into a man a mother is proud to call her son. Thank you for choosing me to be your mom. It's one of my greatest blessings. I will love you forever and always.

To my second (bonus) son, Chase. Even though I didn't give birth to you, I've always considered you my son in every way. I was blessed the day you and your father came into my life, and it's been a pleasure watching you grow into a loving man. I will love you forever and always.

Of course, this book wouldn't be possible without the Ensley family. David, Susanne, Mallory, Leslie, Betty, Jennifer, Sean, Kade, Cole, Randy, Sabra, Katie, Mitch, and to the many extended Ensley, clan. You all have become my family, and I will love you forever and always.

And a special acknowledgment to Liz Williams and Susan Jensen. You both helped me edit chapter after chapter and kept me motivated when needed. Words can't express my thanks and appreciation for all that you've done to help me get this book published. I will love you forever and always.

Dana Cohen, you are my friend and confidant. I'm grateful God brought you into my life. You make me laugh, and you encourage me to continue daring to believe in the impossible. Thank you for reading the book countless times, helping to make it perfect. I will love you forever and always.

And to another special friend, Jessica Magnum. You always believed in me, even from the moment your dog "introduced" us on a walk, and I announced, "I'm writing a book!" You opened my eyes and challenged me to look beyond the obvious and always dare to believe. Thank you, and I will love you forever and always.

My transplant team at Carolinas Medical Center and the all the nurses on the transplant floor—you have my gratitude and appreciation for all that you did to make this experience amazing for me. Thank you!

There have been so many people who have allowed this book to become a reality. You know who you are—thank you and God bless!

Forward

My family and I had just finished dinner when I received a call from my sister, Jennifer Scoggins. She told me that I needed to call a young lady, whom I didn't know. I was shocked and elated as Amy announced to me she was my perfect match for a kidney transplant and that she wanted to give me the precious gift of life.

Diagnosed with Polycystic Kidney Disease (PKD) in 2000, I displayed no symptoms of the disease. In fact, I had gone to the doctor for a completely unrelated issue. In 2009, I was placed on dialysis, and subsequently, the transplant list.

My life and that of my family drastically changed as I began peritoneal dialysis. At night, I attached myself to a machine, and through a tube in my stomach it delivered clean fluid and then drained the waste from my body—essentially acting as an artificial kidney.

Within a year, peritoneal dialysis quit working for my body. I was placed on hemodialysis, and three times a week, I went to a dialysis clinic, which is when my health began to deteriorate.

Jennifer took to Facebook in hopes of finding a donor for me. It worked—Amy found me!

Amy's story is a testament to a life of redemption, faith, and triumph. Her continued commitment to the National Kidney Foundation reflects her character to make a difference.

Miracles do happen—Amy's book is the formula of such a miracle. Through the grace of God, and Amy's courage to believe, she changed the life of a stranger forever.

David Ensley
Amy's Kidney Donation Recipient

Forward

Unless you are a first responder, a practitioner of medicine, or a member of the military, you have probably never had occasion to say, "I saved someone's life today."

This book presents a captivating story where one woman, when given the opportunity to save a life with a living kidney donation, said "Yes!" Told with an endearing sincerity that will both entertain and inform you, Amy doesn't pull any punches about the process of saving a life in this way.

There are lots of factors to consider when making the decision to become a donor. She will capture your heart as she details the adventure and the many unique, intrinsic benefits of choosing to donate life to another human being.

The need for organ donors continues to be outpaced by growing demand. Data from the Organ Procurement and Transplant Network and the US Renal Data System indicate that as of January 2016, there were 121,678 people waiting for organ transplants in the US, and of those, 100,791 were waiting for kidney transplants. On average, over 36,000 people are added to the waitlist each year, and as another point of reference, 17,107 kidney transplants took place in the US in 2014. To further dial up the urgency, 13 people die each day while waiting to receive a kidney transplant.

If you're considering becoming a living donor, or would just like to learn more about organ donation in general, you can find a wide range of resources on the websites for the National Kidney Foundation (www.kidney.org/transplantation), Donate Life America (www.donatelife.net), the Organ Procurement & Transplantation Network (optn.transplant.hrsa.gov or www.organdonor.gov), or the United Network for Organ Sharing (www.unos.org).

Rob Hayden
Executive Director
National Kidney Foundation of the Carolinas

CONTENTS

PART I

CHAPTER ONE 1

CHAPTER TWO 6

CHAPTER THREE 11

CHAPTER FOUR 15

CHAPTER FIVE 18

CHAPTER SIX 24

CHAPTER SEVEN 33

CHAPTER EIGHT 36

CHAPTER NINE 44

CHAPTER TEN 49

CHAPTER ELEVEN 57

CHAPTER TWELVE 63

CHAPTER THIRTEEN 69

PART II

CHAPTER FOURTEEN 75

CHAPTER FIFTEEN 79

CHAPTER SIXTEEN 87

CHAPTER SEVENTEEN	91
CHAPTER EIGHTEEN	97
CHAPTER NINETEEN	102
CHAPTER TWENTY	108
CHAPTER TWENTY-ONE	112
CHAPTER TWENTY-TWO	116

PART III

CHAPTER TWENTY-THREE	120
CHAPTER TWENTY-FOUR	125
CHAPTER TWENTY-FIVE	132
CHAPTER TWENTY-SIX	136
CHAPTER TWENTY-SEVEN	141
CHAPTER TWENTY-EIGHT	148
CHAPTER TWENTY-NINE	152
CHAPTER THIRTY	156
CHAPTER THIRTY-ONE	160
CHAPTER THIRTY-TWO	165
CHAPTER THIRTY-THREE	175
CHAPTER THIRTY-FOUR	182
CHAPTER THIRTY-FIVE	188
CHAPTER THIRTY-SIX	193
CHAPTER THIRTY-SEVEN	196
EPILOGUE	200
ABOUT THE AUTHOR	206
ADDITIONAL RESOURCES	207

PART ONE

CHAPTER ONE

"I have been all things unholy; if God can work through me, he can work through anyone." —St. Francis of Assisi

THE GROOM AND THE BEST MAN took their places at the front of the hall, and the DJ queued the music. All eyes darted to the back of the room. Dressed in an off-white lace gown with flowers in her hair, Mallory appeared with her father by her side. He wore a smile which lit up his face—a moment forever etched in my mind.

The room had been decorated just as in Mallory's childhood dreams. The lights were dimmed, and a sweet fragrance of roses perfumed the air. A spray of white flowers adorned the wedding arch where the couple would speak their vows and cement their life-long commitment with a kiss. But most important of all, the room overflowed with family and friends who came to witness the intimate joining of two precious souls.

Mallory glided by me on the arm of her father looking like a graceful swan streaming through the water. Tears flooded my eyes as I drank in the moment. Mallory's father—tall, healthy, and full of life—beamed with love and admiration for the little girl who had captured his heart many years ago.

Proudly, David Ensley presented his beloved daughter's hand in marriage to the second man she'd ever loved. For both David and Mallory, however, this day proved much more special than simply a happy dad offering his daughter's hand in marriage. For all of us, in fact, it was about savoring a joyful story that could've had a different ending, but thankfully didn't, because of those who dared to believe.

When our new bride, Mallory, was a teenager, her father, David, had been diagnosed with polycystic kidney disease, or PKD, which eventually put him in renal failure. Her wedding day most likely wouldn't have included her father, except that her Aunt Jennifer, desperate for a miracle, had courageously turned to social media.

Jennifer Ensley Scoggins had created a Facebook page, Looking for a Kidney for My Brother David, in hopes of finding a living donor. Neither Jennifer nor their older brother, Randy, were eligible donors, and other family members were not a match. But Jennifer never gave up hope. She believed God would provide a miracle—an angel to help her brother.

Our connection began when Chuck, my husband, casually read Jennifer's Facebook page aloud to me one evening. Something deep within me stirred and with all my heart, I replied, "I hope someone steps up to help him."

My life then took a dramatic 180-degree turn when I heard—from out of nowhere—*"Amy, that person will be you!"*

I had been asking God to use me for His purpose. However, I never thought He'd ask me to do something so outrageous.

On July 6, 2011, I donated a life-saving kidney to David Ensley. It is this fantastic journey that I share with you now.

As an organ donor, I became a perfect match—a 1-in-20 million to be exact—to this man I didn't even know. Our body types were such a close match that we could have been siblings. As a result, David now requires only a small amount of anti-rejection medication to keep his body from rejecting the new kidney I donated.

I initially decided to write this book to educate people about kidney donation and the process I went through. At the time of my surgery, there weren't many books written about the procedure, and I just love books! The ones I found were clinical and boring. I wanted to write about my personal journey with the intent of possibly inspiring others to consider becoming living donors, as well.

The book, however, has evolved into something much more than a story about a kidney donation. It has become a testimonial to daring to believe in the impossible and watching for the synchronicities in life leading you to your divine purpose.

Daring to Believe is an inspiring love story. But most importantly, it's about my ever-growing love affair with God—or "Papa," as I call Him—and discovering that what I've been searching for my entire life was within me all along.

God, Allah, Tao, Source, Adoni, Papa—it doesn't matter how you refer to the Supreme Being of the Universe. God is not a thing, or a place, or a concept. It's the breath within each of us that connects us to the All and to one another.

God is accessible in everyone at any time. You'll find Him in the vagrant on the street or the CEO in the corner office. You'll recognize Him in the act of holding the door for the person behind you or the hug you give a friend. You may or may not find Him in a church or a synagogue or a mosque or a bar, but you will notice Him in the people who frequent those places.

I grew up as a Christian, and you'll find many references to the Christian way of life throughout this book. But I beg you, whether you are Christian or a non-Christian—no matter what your thoughts are about that aspect of your life, please continue reading!

My prayer is that this book touches people across all divides and religions. God is all-encompassing no matter the name He's called!

May you be inspired and Dare to Believe.

CHAPTER TWO

"There's nothing more powerful than an idea whose time has come." — Victor Hugo

IT WAS THREE-THIRTY ON THE MORNING of July 6, 2011. The alarm shrilled. I had been staring at the ceiling for hours, as if dreaming with my eyes wide-open. I reached over to silence the noise, and a wide grin spread across my face.

Today was the day I'd been anticipating for months. All the testing, questions, and endless conversations had led to this moment. Today, I would donate my kidney to David Ensley, a man who, before this decision, I had never met. Today, God would use me for His miracle. Today, we were saving a life—David Ensley's life.

I hopped out of bed and scrambled to the bathroom to brush my teeth. I wasn't allowed to eat breakfast or even enjoy my beloved morning coffee, but I would, at least, have fresh breath and clean teeth.

I yelled to my motionless husband, Chuck, "Honey, let's get going. Out of bed!"

He mumbled, "I'm getting up," and tried to pull the blankets back over this head.

"Now," I commanded. How could he even think of sleeping in today? I wondered, shaking my head in disbelief.

"I'm up. I'm up," he said kicking off the blankets as his feet hit the floor.

"Good," I muttered, "I don't want to be late." Although if we were late for anything, it usually wasn't because of Chuck. He had an annoying habit of always being 10 minutes early for everything. But today I must be early.

I pulled on blue striped shorts and a white cotton T-shirt I had laid out the night before. I wanted casual and comfortable. Remembering instructions not to bring anything valuable, I placed my wedding rings in the top drawer of my jewelry box for safe keeping. I hadn't removed these rings since our wedding day, two years before.

Although, Chuck and I had only married two years earlier on September 26, 2009, our love story began twenty years before as high school sweethearts. As my first love, I can still remember the first time I laid eyes on him.

My brother, James, and I were walking to the store when this old, dirty, brown Mustang pulled up beside us. Chuck, with a tan arm hanging out the window, asked if we needed a ride. We locked eyes, and as he smiled, the rest of the world vanished. He was beautiful. I blushed, and the air crackled with electricity around me.

I sat in the back seat, and Chuck positioned the rearview mirror to glance at me from time to time, as he and my brother talked. I didn't dare say anything for fear of words such as, "You're beautiful. I love you. We'd make gorgeous babies," escaping from my mouth.

Chuck dropped us off at the store and asked if he could wait to drive us home. James began to say, "No…" but I quickly interrupted, "Yes. Thank you." He drove us home and we saw each other every day after that for the next two years.

I always knew we would marry one day, and often told him, even back then. I just never thought it would take a lifetime to get him down the aisle.

Neither one of us really remembers why we broke up in high school, but I have a suspicion it had something to do with the blonde girl I saw him with at a restaurant, not long afterward.

He and I reconnected on Facebook twenty years later through the East Mecklenburg High School Twenty-Year Reunion page for the class of 1989. I sent him a friend request.

When we met again, it was as if we had never separated. I called to ask him to help a friend of mine who had to move out of the house she and her husband shared. Chuck dropped everything—no questions asked. Our first "date" in over twenty years, and he moved furniture which wasn't even mine.

We were older now, with more wrinkles and heavier baggage, but he still had those luscious lips I loved to devour, and deep, brown eyes which held my attention for hours.

Over the years, many points of intersection had occurred in our lives, as though the universe had been pulling strings to keep us close until we were ready to connect.

For several years, we both worked in the same bank building in uptown. We were on separate floors and employed by different companies, but somehow, we never ran into each other on the elevators or even in the coffee shop on the main level. We also worked in adjacent buildings in another local complex, and again, never bumped into each other even in the parking lot.

But probably the biggest surprise of all was when we discovered we lived only a few hundred feet from each other. From my garage, I had an excellent view of Chuck's patio, though I didn't know it was his.

Also, we each had a son from previous relationships. The boys knew each other from junior high school and rode the same bus. They even looked similar—tall, with blonde hair and blue eyes, and both were born in June but one year apart.

God's ways are miraculous to me. He knew when Chuck and I were dating in high school that we were perfect for each other. We just needed more refining before He brought us back together. He kept our lives parallel throughout the years, no matter what we were experiencing, as if to keep us forever connected.

Sometimes I wondered if Chuck and I hadn't reconnected, would I have met David or heard about his story? Chuck had been long-time friends with David's sister, Jennifer, and his older brother, Randy. Because of their friendships, I found out about David's need for a kidney.

And now, here we are—driving to the hospital today because I was David's 1-in-20 million miracle—his perfect match.

CHAPTER THREE

"God is love, and he who abides in love abides in God, and God in him." —1 John 4:16

WE DROVE PEACEFULLY, SURROUNDED BY the deepest quiet I've ever known. The roads were deserted; not too many people are out at 4:30 in the morning. The sun would rise soon with its colors of lavender and radiant amber, but I wouldn't see its beauty on this particular morning.

I looked at Chuck, and he reached over to caress my hand, allowing his fingers to linger for a moment, his faced etched with worry. I could tell he preferred to reflect on his own thoughts in silence, leaving me to stare out into the silky blackness of the early morning.

My mind looped back to how this very unusual experience all began. It had been a normal day, like any other. I had worked and visited with my brother and his family, who lived behind us in another town home. I had cooked dinner—just an everyday normal routine. But that day had altered my life forever.

As I cleaned the kitchen, Chuck had called to me from the living room.

"Honey, do you remember Jennifer Ensley from high school?"

I thought about it for a second and replied, "Nope. Doesn't ring a bell. Should I?"

"We all went to East Mecklenburg together," he replied, as though it was supposed to make a difference to me. I peered from the kitchen and shook my head.

"Well, I'm sure you'd remember her if you ever saw her again. Randy, her brother, got me the job at the Speedway as a security guard."

"Oh, yeah!" I still didn't remember her or her brother, but I did remember the job. I hated it because Chuck wasn't around for my birthday. The Coca-Cola 600 was the second week in May along with my birthday.

"What does Jennifer Ensley have to do with anything?" I asked.

"I'm looking at a Facebook page she started called, 'Looking for a Kidney for My Brother David,'" he said. Interesting, I thought.

Chuck continued on, telling me that David, the middle child in that family, had married his high school sweetheart, Susanne.

They had two girls, Mallory, who was in nursing school, and Leslie, a senior in high school.

Diagnosed with polycystic kidney disease in 2000, David was now in complete renal failure and on dialysis but would die if he didn't receive a kidney transplant soon. This was the reason Jennifer had created the Facebook page.

I pondered the story. My heart broke for those girls and his wife. I lost my father several years back, and I knew firsthand the pain of losing a parent. I would give anything to have my dad back.

"Wow," I said. "How sad. I hope someone steps up to help him."

Then I heard it. It was as audible as if I were talking with someone right in front of me. The Voice said, "Amy, that person will be you." An intense tingling sensation ran down my spine and burned within my soul. Instantaneously, I knew I would be David's donor.

I remember looking around the kitchen and screaming in my mind, "Um, excuse me? WHAT did you say? Where did that Voice come from?" I wondered.

I have heard about people hearing things from God, but never considered it would happen to me, much less in the middle of cleaning up the kitchen after dinner.

Although I have "felt" things before that I knew in my heart were from God, I'd never actually heard Him, as if in conversation.

The Voice didn't sound as I imagined "His" voice would sound—if, in fact, He would have an actual voice. It sounded like my tone and inflection. Yet, somehow, I knew God had spoken to me.

I was young in my faith, but my trust in God was growing. I had recently been praying, asking God to use me for His purpose, but donating a body part, I thought, that was too much to ask. Wasn't it?

Instead of telling Chuck, or anyone, I decided not to share my new revelation, at least not yet. I kept quiet, afraid Chuck would think I was kind of crazy and would want to send me to the proverbial ditch he often jokes with me about. Besides, I wasn't too sure about what had just happened, myself.

CHAPTER FOUR

"Give light and the darkness will disappear itself."
—Desiderius Erasmus

WE ARRIVED AT THE HOSPITAL that morning at 4:45 a.m. and checked in at the front desk. The receptionist, a small, older lady with grayish hair, pointed to a small room off to the right and asked us to wait there. "Someone will be down to escort you to the pre-op waiting room soon," she said.

As directed, Chuck and I moved into the small room. The room was completely barren except for a few cushioned blue chairs lining the walls and one TV hanging on the wall in the corner. The local news station had just started broadcasting the morning's news—except the TV had no sound, just words scrolling on the bottom of the screen.

Since we were the only people there, we had our choice of where to sit. Chuck picked a seat against the wall of windows, and I took the one beside him. I turned and looked out into the lightless morning. Doctors and nurses meandered in from the parking deck, and a janitor mopped the entrance floor. Then, he laid out the day's welcome mat. Still quiet, the hospital slowly began awakening from its dreams.

As we waited to hear my name called, I wondered if David had arrived yet. Of course, he had, I thought. David's always early for everything. Like Chuck, they both lived by the motto, "If I'm not at least fifteen minutes early, then, I'm late!" Personally, as long as I wasn't more than fifteen minutes late, than I considered myself on time—the perfect catalyst for a few annoying arguments between me and Chuck.

I smiled as I remembered the first time I had spoken with David. Almost immediately, we felt a sense of familiarity and comfort between us. It was as if we had known each other our entire lives.

I had passed all the other tests and only the MRI remained which determined the kidney the doctors would use. But, since the test was expensive, they wanted to know David's opinion before moving any further.

Chuck had found the home number for Jennifer, David's sister, online, and called her. Sean, her husband, answered the phone. Chuck explained he'd known Jennifer from high school, and he had some important news he needed to tell her; could he please speak with her? Uneasy about a strange man calling his wife, Sean asked, "Can I tell her what this is about?"

"It's about David," and then, Chuck gave Sean our home number and hung up.

Jennifer called Chuck back within twenty minutes. He told Jennifer about how I had felt called to get tested as David's donor and as it turned out we were a match. The doctors told us to find out if David had any objections about moving forward with me.

"Sweet Jesus, no, he doesn't!" Jennifer exclaimed.

Chuck hung up the phone, not giving me a chance to talk. I gave Chuck an inquisitive look and he responded, "Jennifer will call David and have him call right back."

About thirty minutes later, the phone rang a second time. Chuck answered and then handed me the phone. As I walked out onto our patio I said, "Hello."

CHAPTER FIVE

"All the darkness in the world can not extinguish the light of one candle." — St. Francis of Assisi

AN AFRICAN-AMERICAN MAN IN GREEN scrubs with a big, toothy grin appeared in the doorway of the waiting room. "Amy Gray-Cunningham?" I looked at him and signaled it was me. Here we go, I thought.

He introduced himself as Michael and told me he would escort me to the pre-op waiting room. Then he grabbed my wrist to read the hospital bracelet I received the week before at my pre-op appointment and asked my name and date of birth. It struck me as funny that I had to answer the question when it was clearly printed on the bracelet. But I gave it anyway, "Amy Gray-Cunningham and May 13, 1970."

Michael must have read my mind because his voice contained a hint of humor when he said, "You better get used to answering that question. You'll be asked it every time a nurse or doctor enters the room."

I smiled back and shrugged, "No problem. Just seems redundant is all."

"I know. Are you ready to go?"

"Without a doubt," I said.

Chuck grabbed my bag and we followed Michael down the corridor to the elevators behind the reception desk. As he pushed the button for the elevators, he said, "Once we get to the waiting room, you can have a seat until they're ready for you in pre-op."

I nodded. The elevator doors rattled opened.

Glancing at my husband with my overnight bag in his hand, his eyes glimmered with love. Smiling, I thought about the night I told him my desire to get tested as David's donor. Exasperated, he assumed I had finally lost it.

After Chuck told me about Jennifer's Facebook page, I couldn't get David's story and what I had heard out of my mind. Several times, I secretly logged into Chuck's Facebook account, so I could follow Jennifer's updates. After reading that David was O positive, I decided it was time to complete a donor application. I, too, was O positive.

Telling Chuck about my decision, however, was more complicated than I anticipated. At dinner, I finally found the nerve to tell him.

"Honey I've been thinking, and I want to get tested to see if I'm a match for David Ensley."

Chuck looked up at me from his dinner plate and with a glaring eye, said, "You what?"

"I admit it's crazy."

"Crazy?" he interrupted.

Perturbed by his comment, I continued, "I feel I'm being led to do this. Besides, the chances I'm a match are slim. But I know it's something I'm supposed to do."

Dropping the fork to his plate, Chuck pushed back his chair and questioned, "And what makes you think this is something you're SUPPOSED to do?"

I had already decided it was best not to tell him I heard God talking to me, telling me I was the one. Instead I said, "I haven't been able to get his story out of my mind. It's all I can think about. I even went on your Facebook page to follow Jennifer's posts."

Irritated, he said, "YOU DID WHAT?" annunciating each syllable.

"Oh, come on," I replied, gulping my wine for courage. "You gave me your password, and it's not like I haven't done it in the past. I wanted to follow what Jennifer posted, but I didn't want to "like" the page, yet. The most recent post said, David is O positive and, Chuck, I'm O positive. For me, it was a clear sign."

"Who cares? It doesn't mean you need to do this."

"You said it yourself, if someone doesn't step up, he could die. He has two daughters, and if I can help him dance with his daughters at their weddings, I want to. No, I need to do this. Besides, I've been researching kidney donation, and if for whatever reason I needed a kidney in the future, then, I move to the top of the donor list for a new one."

"Well, just wonderful! But, what if one our boys needs a kidney? Have you thought about how you would feel if you weren't able to give them one because you gave one to someone you don't even know?" he asked.

I looked into Chuck's eyes and grabbed his hand. I needed to make him understand. "I just have to believe and have faith God will provide for them. I can't decide not to do this based on something which may or may not happen in the future. How selfish would I be?"

Chuck looked away—not because he didn't have anything more to say. He just knew it would be pointless. The next day I called the Transplant Clinic to request an application.

The lady who answered the phone at the clinic had a soft, gentle voice: "And who would you like the application for?"

"David Ensley," I replied.

"May I ask how you know Mr. Ensley?"

For a moment, I considered my reply because I wasn't prepared to answer the question. What would she think if I told her David was a stranger? I decided to be honest and said, "David's a high school friend of my husband but I don't know him. Will it be a problem?"

"Oh, no," she replied, "I think it's wonderful you're willing to get tested. Not many people are as compassionate. It's just a question we have to ask."

At least she didn't think of me as crazy. She told me she would mail the packet immediately and I should receive it within the week. I said, "Thank you," and hung up the phone. Now all I had to do was wait.

I muttered a quick prayer, *"Papa, I've done as You've asked. Now it's in Your capable hands. Thank You."*

Just as the lady from the clinic had promised, I received the application packet within a few days. Putting all the other mail under my arm, I attempted to open the packet while walking into the house.

I thumbed through the information when the front door opened and Maggie, our German Shepherd, barked with excitement. Assuming Chuck had come in, I yelled from the kitchen, "Hey, honey."

He came around the corner with Maggie at his heels and bent over to give me a quick kiss. "Hello! What's this?" he asked referring to the packet in my hands.

"It's the donor application," I said with a smile, as I held up the thick packet for him to see. "At a glance, I have a feeling it'll take me a while to answer everything. The questions seem very detailed." Feeling discouraged, I laid it on the counter and then turned and opened the refrigerator.

As he slipped his arms around my waist and nuzzled my neck, Chuck said, "Well, I haven't changed my mind. I still don't want you to do it, but I must admit, I'm proud of you for considering it."

A much different response from the other night when I told him I was thinking about doing this, I mused.

"I love you," I said patting his arms, still around my waist. "And, thank you."

"You know," he whispered in my ear, "If it meant I could save you from having to go through an unnecessary surgery, I would send in an application, but they would never approve me, not with diabetes."

His words warmed me and made me feel safe in his arms. I turned to look at him and replied, "Thank you for wanting to protect me, but it's in God's hands, not ours. This is not something I have to do. It's something I feel led to do. Does it make any sense?" I asked. I wished I could make him understand, but how could I, when I had a hard time comprehending it myself.

"Somewhat, I guess. But I still don't like it," he muttered.

"I know, and besides, I may not even get approved. They may take one look at my application and say it's not happening. Now, let me get dinner ready. Maggie still needs to go for her walk."

"OK," he said, swatting my butt before grabbing the leash.

CHAPTER SIX

"Trust in the dreams, for in them is hidden the gate to eternity." — Kahlil Gibran (The Prophet)

THE ELEVATOR DOORS SLID OPEN. We followed Michael down a long, beige hallway to another waiting room. My nose crinkled at the sterile disinfectant in the air. Entering the waiting room, Michael gestured to us to take a seat and said, "Someone will be out to get you soon."

"Thank you," Chuck said.

This room, larger and more spacious than the first, was equipped with a Starbucks coffee station and several snack machines. Oh, what I wouldn't give for a Skinny Vanilla Latte! In the middle, a large fresh water fish aquarium provided an atmosphere of peace and tranquility. The blue-cushioned chairs, strategically scattered in squared sections, provided privacy for families waiting on news of their loved ones. Flat screen T.V.'s hung near each area but only a couple of them were turned on. I looked to the left and saw Chuck's sister, Fran, waving us over.

I couldn't believe my in-laws were there already. It wasn't even 5:00 in the morning. "Thank you for being here but you didn't have to come, especially this early."

My mother-in-law, in her late seventies had two hip replacement surgeries and relied on a walker to get around. For them to get to the hospital as early as they did was an accomplishment, and I loved them so much for it.

Granna, Chuck's mother replied, "Where else would we be?" Beside her sat a bag of snacks, bottles of water, crossword puzzles, books and a pink blanket across her lap. She looked settled in for the day.

Chuck's family had been incredibly supportive. Of course, they were apprehensive at first, but eventually they relented and offered their unwavering support– no questions asked.

"Are you nervous?" Fran asked.

"Surprisingly, no. I can't believe it's actually happening, but I've never been surer about anything in my life. Does that make any sense?"

I knew it sounded crazy because I wasn't nervous. I thought I should be and part of me felt the need to apologize. I just knew in my heart everything would work out. Besides, Chuck and my mother were nervous enough for everyone.

I love my mother. She's my heroine and mentor. She raised

my brother, sister and me alone and never gave up on any of us—even me when I made life difficult for her. Admittedly, I wasn't an easy child and I put her through hell on many occasions, but I always knew I could count on her. Today wasn't any different.

As if on cue, I noticed my mom and step-father at the front desk. I waved. "Mom, over here."

Mom had recently retired, after forty years of nursing, to take care of my step-father, Terry, who had suffered a stroke and needed her at home. Retirement looked good on her. She had always been slim, but she looked as though she had lost a few pounds and had a hint of color on her face. She had decided to quit coloring her hair, some time ago, and now her strawberry-blonde hair was peppered with grayish-white.

"They haven't called you back, yet? I worried we'd get here late and miss seeing you."

"I'm expecting them to call me at any moment. Perfect timing!"

Just then a tornado-like force bounded into the waiting room. I laughed at the energy that Jennifer, David's sister, created. Constantly moving and talking, she commanded the attention of everyone in the room.

In her early 40's and mother of two spirited boys, Jennifer never surrendered her quest to find a perfect match for her brother. In 2000, David was diagnosed with PKD and nine years later he went into complete renal failure. The doctors put him on a home dialysis system, called Peritoneal Dialysis. Then, after a year it suddenly quit working.

As a result, he was taken off the transplant list and put on Hemodialysis in hopes of getting him back to an acceptable level for a transplant. Hemodialysis meant he had to drive to a clinic several times a week for a machine to clean the toxins from his blood. He no longer had the freedom to do it at home.

Eventually, some of the cysts on his kidneys ruptured, causing even more adversity for David and his family. Jennifer feared if he didn't receive a new kidney soon, they would lose him, which led her to create the Facebook page to save his life. She heard God's voice and without her unbelievable faith in God and her love for her brother, all of this would not have been happening here today.

"Amy-Angel," she cried out. "Give me a hug." She pulled me in and almost squeezed the air out of me. Amy-Angel, as she affectionately called me, was a name I wasn't too keen on.

"How are you, sweet girl?" she asked, but then turned to hug the next person, not waiting for an answer.

Betty Ensley, her mother, came in behind her. I loved this woman. She had the most generous spirit. She looked like most grandmothers with grayish, white hair and a petite frame. She also had polycystic kidney disease and since the disease is hereditary, there's a strong possibility David inherited it from Betty. She obviously was not a viable candidate to give her son a kidney and, personally, I thought it hurt her deeply.

Betty hugged me and looked as if she wanted to say something, but choked up, instead.

Just then I heard my name, "Amy Gray-Cunningham," from somewhere in the front of the room. I looked for Chuck, and he immediately took my side.

"I guess this is it." I looked around the room, grateful for all the support, as I pressed back tears.

A nurse appeared and said to my family, "As soon as I get her settled in at Pre-op, I'll let you all know. You can see her before they take her back to surgery."

She looked at Chuck, who was holding tightly to my hand. "And it includes you, too. I'll be back to get you shortly."

Standing on my tip-toes, I gave him a tender kiss, "Love you."

"Love you, too."

As I walked down the long corridor with the nurse and two other people scheduled for surgeries, I thought to myself how a few weeks ago I didn't think we would be here. At that time, David's doctor had rejected me as his donor.

I vividly remembered the call I received from Tania, my transplant coordinator, telling me I wasn't approved. My heart leaped as I saw her number flash on my phone. I was in an unexpected Friday afternoon meeting and couldn't take her call. Reluctantly, I punched the end button and sent her to voicemail.

As soon as the meeting ended, I walked outside to the parking lot for a little privacy to call her back. I hadn't told anyone at work about my decision to donate a kidney, and I didn't want to be overheard.

I redialed the last missed call, "Hello, Tania. It's Amy Cunningham. I'm sorry I missed your call?"

"Oh, hi, Amy. Thank you for calling me back."

My stomach clenched. I could tell from her voice I didn't want to hear what she was about to tell me.

"I have some unfortunate news," she said.

She proceeded to tell me that David's doctor had decided the surgery would be too risky. The MRI showed both my kidneys had an extra, tiny artery on the top of each. Typically, it wouldn't be a problem, but mine were so tiny that the doctor was afraid he wouldn't be able to reattach it. As a result, he couldn't confirm how much kidney function would be lost. David could lose 10, 20, or even 30 percent and in that case, it would cause him more harm than good.

Tania continued, "And another potential donor has submitted an application. David's doctor wants to pursue it to determine if this person would be a better match for David."

Speechless, my lower lip quivered, as I fought back tears. Since the night in my kitchen when I first found out about David, I knew this was what I was supposed to do. *Why, Papa? What's been the purpose, if not to be David's donor?*

"I thought the review committee gave me the approval, and we were only waiting for a surgery date?"

"Your doctors approved you, but David's doctor still needed to give his blessing, and he feels it would be too risky."

"Wow, okay. Where do we go from here?"

"I will talk with this new applicant and get the process started. If this person is not a good candidate, then the team may come back to you, if you're still interested."

"I understand and yes, of course, I'm still interested."

All I wanted was for David to be well again, but I felt disappointed it wouldn't be me to help him. I believed with everything in me this was God's plan for me, and now I doubted myself and my faith after one phone call. At least there was another possible donor who may be an even better match.

Then, out of nowhere I asked, "Since I'm approved to be a donor, could I donate to someone else or will this extra little artery prevent me from donating to anyone?"

Maybe God's intent was not to use me to heal David but someone else altogether. Maybe I still heard Him correctly, but He used David—someone I 'sort of' knew—to acclimate me to this crazy idea of kidney donation.

To me, this sounded like a conceivable theory, and one God would surely accept. I nodded in approval as I resolved this matter in my head.

"No, it won't prevent you from donating to someone else

but just as with David's doctor, another doctor might feel it's too risky, as well. Let's wait and see what happens, and we can discuss it at another time."

"Okay, but please keep me posted."

"I will, and Amy, thank you. You're doing a good thing."

"Thanks," I said and pressed the end button on the phone.

Instinctively, I dialed David's number.

He answered with a bark, "I just heard, and its bullshit! I have an appointment with Dr. Kendal next week, and I'm demanding we move forward with you."

A smiled broke across my face. David didn't mince words. He did, however, love to talk, especially if he was voicing his opinion about a particular politician he didn't agree with at the moment, or about the government in general. He could always make me laugh with his outrageous commentary on how the government needs to be fixed and about those who serve as our fearless political leaders.

Attempting to sound positive, I said, "David, Tania told me there was another person who could be a compatible donor for you. Don't you think you should wait to see who it is and if he or she may be a better match for you..."

"Not possible," David interrupted. "God brought you into my life for a reason. You're MY miracle."

"Thank you, David, but I was just denied as your donor."

"We'll just see about it," he said, and then the line went dead.

I sat there on the curb absently staring at the cars in the parking lot. Unfortunately, this was not the news I was expecting, yet I remained hopeful. God would work it out. We had a plan, right?

CHAPTER SEVEN

"Ask and it will be given to you; seek and you will find; knock and the door will be opened to you. For everyone who asks receives; the one who seeks finds; and to the one who knocks, the door will be opened." —Matthew 7:7-8

THE FOLLOWING MONDAY, CHUCK AND I met Jennifer and her husband, Sean, at our church for a healing service. We had previously arranged to attend before the news on Friday and decided to go anyway. David didn't come because he was too sick.

Sadly, this was the first time Chuck and I had attended a healing service in the two years that we had been members of the church. Jennifer commented she'd never been to one at her church, either. We were willing to try anything because David's health was rapidly declining, and he needed a new kidney as soon as possible.

Jennifer, however, said she didn't care what the doctor said, and exclaimed, "We are declaring and praying it into existence!" I admired her passion but didn't understand it. I thought she was demanding too much of God because His will would prevail, regardless. But she believed in His promises: *"If you believe, you will receive whatever you ask for in prayer."* (Matthew 21:22)

And believing is what happened: we declared it; prayed it into existence, and it became our reality.

In the dimly lit sanctuary, people sat in quietest reflection. The music swirled around the room, a meditative melody. We found a seat toward the back as a minister began reciting scriptures on healing, while someone strummed lightly on the guitar.

"...and the blind and the lame came to him in the temple, and he healed them." (Matthew 21:14)

Then Jesus answered her, *"O woman, great is your faith! Be it done for you as you desire."* (Matthew 15:28)

As the minister continued to recite healing scripture, people made their way to the front for laying-on-of-hands and personal prayers from a prayer team member.

We waited for the opportunity to pray with Chris Thayer, a good friend of Chuck's and one of the ministers of the church. We told Chris the condensed version of our story and how David couldn't be with us because he was too sick. Chris instructed me and Jennifer to sit in chairs facing each other, our knees barely touching as we held hands.

Chris and his wife, Terry, laid their hands on us, and then asked Chuck and Sean to do the same. Chris prayed, and to be honest, I don't remember what was said or what happened. I entered a deep meditative trance as a brilliant feeling of love enveloped me. I felt as if I had left my body and floated through the heavens, while God and His angels worked miracles.

I left the church with a renewed perspective. I believed in my soul that God would heal David with my kidney. Three days later on June 9th, David and I were approved for surgery. The surgeon just changed his mind, and three weeks later as I walked to the pre-op room, I murmured, *"Thank you, Papa!"*

CHAPTER EIGHT

"And still, after all this time, The sun never says to the earth, "You owe Me." Look what happens with a love like that, It lights the Whole Sky." —**Hafez**"

THE NURSE PRESSED A METAL button on the wall marked "Doors Open." The heavy, double doors parted, providing a large pathway as we entered the pre-op room. "Amy, wait here. I'll be right back," she said, pointing to a corner by the nurses' station, and then motioned for the other two people to follow her.

I nodded and pulled my sweater tighter around me. The cool temperature in the hospital caused goose bumps to prickle up over my skin. I was grateful Chuck reminded me to bring the sweater.

Laughter spilled from the nurse's station. I wished I could've heard the joke, but it didn't matter. Standing alone in the pre-op room, listening to the chatter and watching the nurses move from behind one curtained bed to another, a wave of uneasiness came over me.

Which curtain guarded David? Jennifer told me he was here when I saw her in the waiting room. I felt nervous but not for me. If this surgery didn't work, then David wouldn't get another chance—this was it for him.

The nurse came back and said, "Okay. We're going over there," and ushered me into an empty holding area which contained a metal gurney with a thin mattress, a reclining chair and brown, laminate cabinets with a counter top and a small sink. A large curtain hung from tracks in the ceiling, so it could glide from the back wall to the side wall, providing privacy for my make-shift room.

Pulling open one of the cabinet doors, the nurse turned and handed me an ugly bluish-green checkered gown along with a small, plastic package of bright yellow socks with treads on both sides. She instructed me to take off my clothes, including my underwear and bra and put on the gown and socks.

"My name is Beth. You can put your belongings in this bag. Call for me if you need anything. I'll be at the nurses' station and will be back shortly." She grabbed the curtain and pulled it closed.

As I put on the bright yellow socks, I thought about the first call I received from Tania a few weeks after submitting my donor application. I was in Chicago at a trade show. The show floor reverberated with loud noises as people hustled from one booth to another. Directly across from my booth was the show's networking lounge. Crowds would gather to charge their cell phones or watch the news on the flat-screen TVs. This area of the floor bustled with constant commotion; hearing my cell phone ring was a miracle in itself.

I saw a Charlotte area code pop up on the display. I thought about letting the call go to voicemail and calling back at a better time, but I didn't want to miss the call if it was the clinic.

To hear better, I buried my finger in my open ear and pressed the phone hard against the other. "Hello, this is Amy Cunningham."

The voice on the other end replied, "Hello, Amy. I'm Tania Summers with the Charlotte Transplant Clinic. Is now a good time to talk?"

Surveying my surroundings, I shrugged and said, "Yes, as long as you don't mind some background noise. I'm at a trade show, and unfortunately, it's loud."

I went behind a tall, black curtain toward the bathrooms, hoping to find quiet and more privacy.

"I can call you another time if you prefer," she replied.

"No, no, it's okay. I have a few minutes. Thank you for calling me."

"We received your donor application, and I'd like to ask you a few questions. Your application is for David Ensley. How do you know him?"

There was the dreaded question I feared the most. Would she think I was crazy? I didn't know David and yet wanted to give him a kidney—sounded weird even to me.

"Well, um, I don't technically know him." I stammered. "My husband, Chuck, knew his sister, Jennifer, in high school, and met him a few times growing up. Jennifer created a Facebook page called, *'Looking for a Kidney for My Brother David'* and that is how I found out about him and his need for a kidney."

I imagined Tania shaking her head in disbelief and wondering what she could say to get off the phone with me as fast as possible. Instead, she asked, "What does your husband think about you submitting a donor application for David?"

"Well, to be honest, Chuck wasn't too pleased with it at first, but I explained I wanted to see if I would be a match for David. I told him the likelihood of it was slim, but I felt a huge need to find out. It's more like a calling."

For a brief moment, I considered telling her about the night I heard of David's story and the Voice telling me I would be the one to give him a kidney. Luckily, I decided against it out of fear that she would think I was crazier than I already appeared.

"Not too many people would do what you've done and submit an application, so thank you. Let me ask you, how do you think your husband would feel if you're approved?"

I breathed in deeply. "I'm not sure, but we'll work it out if it happens. My husband loves me, and he'll support my decision either way."

"Good. I needed to ask. Before we go any further, are you being forced in any way or expecting to receive financial reimbursement for your kidney?"

"No! Absolutely not. I want to do this of my free will and I don't expect compensation in any way." I couldn't believe she had asked me this question.

Sensing my annoyance, she replied, "Please understand. I'm legally required to ask. Receiving compensation for a kidney is illegal. I had to ask even though I knew what your answer would be. Thank you for your honesty."

She continued, "I want you to understand submitting an application in no way requires you to move forward with the donation process. Anytime you want to stop, just tell me, and it's done. No one will ever have to know. Clear?"

"I understand. I want to move forward."

"Perfect. Let's continue then," Tania said. "So, your blood type is O positive—good. Do you smoke?"

"No."

"Do you drink?"

"Yes, occasionally."

"Perfect. From your application, I see you are about 5'2" and weigh about 145. Have you ever had any other surgeries?" she asked.

"Yes, I had my appendix removed about four years ago."

"Any complications?"

"No, not that I can remember. Although I did wake up in the middle of the surgery... otherwise, no complications."

"Wow, sounds frightening. The next step, if you're interested, is to come in for some blood work. We cross-match your blood with David's to see if there are any antibodies present which would cause his body to reject your kidney. The lower the antibodies, the closer the match. We will also test your creatinine level, which tells us how well your kidneys function. There are other things we test for, like hepatitis and HIV, but the creatinine level and the crossmatch are the most important. If it comes back that you are a match for David and your kidneys are functioning well, then I would have you come in and meet with me for more extensive testing. Would you like to move forward?"

"Oh, yes, definitely."

"What about David? Have you told him yet what your plans are?"

"No, we haven't. Can we wait to tell him until or if there's more definite news to give him? I don't want to get his hopes up to have him disappointed." Besides, I thought to myself; I didn't even know his phone number.

"I understand. We don't need to say anything right now, but

eventually if you do get approved, you might want to consider telling him."

I let her words sink in for a minute. How would I tell him if I was approved? What would he think? He doesn't know me. What if he freaks out? Oh Papa, have I gone crazy?

Tania, as if reading my mind, followed up with, "This type of thing doesn't happen all the time where someone you don't know generously gives you a kidney. I'm sure he will be amazed at your kindness. You will have a friend for life."

"Thank you, Tania."

"When will you be back in town?" she asked.

"I get back on Saturday."

"Can you stop by Monday morning to give the blood and urine samples? You can do it before work, so you don't miss anything, if you're still interested."

"Oh, yes; most definitely," I replied, feeling a bit perturbed that she continued asking me if I was still interested. Hadn't I already said I was interested? I submitted an application; doesn't it mean I'm interested? However, I would soon find out that she would ask me this question every time I'd speak with her.

"Good. You won't need to see me. Just let the receptionist know you're there for blood work, and I'll have your paperwork ready for you with the phlebotomist."

"How long will it take to get the results back?" I asked.

"Not long. We should have an answer by the end of the week at the latest."

"Wow, quick. Okay. Perfect. I'll be there on Monday. Can you email me the address?" I asked, realizing I didn't have a pen on me.

"Sure. And again, thank you, Amy. You are doing a great thing!"

"Thanks," I said and ended the call.

I leaned up against the brick wall next to the women's bathroom and closed my eyes. It's happening. But I'm sure once they get the blood work back, it won't go any further. I was healthy now, but I spent years as a reckless teenager, consuming drugs and alcohol. It would take a miracle for me to be a desirable match.

Thinking about my life back then unnerved me. It felt like there had been a stranger in my skin. I didn't believe in God or, at least, I didn't believe He cared about me. I had no respect for others, much less for myself. I did what I wanted when I wanted. Smoking pot and using cocaine were a way of life. Stealing, manipulating and conning people were my hobbies.

It wasn't until I was given the gift of motherhood that I came to believe in unconditional love and in something outside of myself which was far greater than me. Staring into the eyes of my beautiful baby, I instinctively knew I would love him forever, no matter what happened. He changed me from the inside out.

CHAPTER NINE

"Attitude is a choice. Happiness is a choice. Optimism is a choice. Kindness is a choice. Giving is a choice. Respect is a choice. Whatever choice you make makes you. Choose wisely."
—Roy T. Bennett (The Light in the Heart)

WHEN I RETURNED TO MY hotel room, I called Chuck to fill him in on my conversation with Tania. I heard a long, uncomfortable silence on his end.

"What does it mean? Does she think you're a match?" he asked.

"I don't know. We have the same blood type, and one of the tests is to see if my blood, when mixed with David's, produces antibodies, which may cause him to reject my kidney. Tania said the lower the antibodies, the better." I paused to let the information settle in and then continued, "She said she will know more after the blood work comes back."

"How long will it take?"

"She said we'll know something by the end of the week."

"Okay, I love you. Talk to you in the morning," he muttered.

"Love you too." The line went silent.

I knew Chuck had a hard time with my decision, but this was something I needed to do. Besides, the likelihood David and I would be a match was slim. Chuck had nothing to worry about; I was certain. But deep inside, I trusted the Voice I heard—David and I would be a perfect match.

The following Monday I got up an hour early, so I could stop by the transplant clinic to provide the blood and urine samples on my way into work. As promised, Tania emailed me the address along with a few pamphlets about living organ donation.

I read that people who received kidneys from a living donor had a better rate of survival than those who received cadaver kidneys—a kidney from someone who has died. The living donated kidney spends less time outside of the body and starts working faster than a cadaver kidney.

I arrived at the clinic promptly at 8 a.m. and checked in with the receptionist. I glanced around the room and watched as several people shifted uncomfortably in hard, plastic chairs not designed for long periods of sitting. They looked disheveled and tired and radiated a weird gray aura. My heart sank as I wondered why they were there. Did they have kidney disease? Were they waiting for dialysis? Or was it their family member who was sick and they were waiting for them?

Did David look like them? Could he be sitting in this room? I didn't even know what he looked like, and yet, I wanted to donate my kidney to him. Was I crazy? It couldn't be normal or rational thinking. But yet, here I stood, surrounded by the brokenness of kidney disease, and my heart wept for them and for David.

Silently, I lifted up a quick prayer, *"Papa, please help me and these people in this room. I ask you for healing and comfort."* Then the receptionist snapped me out of my thoughts.

"Okay, you're all ready. Just sign in on the clipboard by the next door and have a seat in the waiting room. Someone will be with you shortly."

I nodded as I grabbed the paperwork she handed me and went to sign in as instructed. I was third on the list. Good. It shouldn't be too long.

I sat nervously in the seat closest to the door of the room, waiting to hear my name called. I wanted to run away. Honestly, this had to be the most absurd thing I'd ever thought of doing. What made me think I would be the one to save this man's life because I heard a voice in my head?

I could just slip out the front door before my name was called, and no one will ever know. Chuck would be thrilled, and I could go on with my life as though nothing had ever happened.

But then, I remembered, *"Amy you are the one."* Damn! So, I waited.

Just then I heard, "Mrs. Gray-Cunningham?" I looked up, and a tall, slender man with wide almond-shaped eyes dressed in white scrubs stood in the doorway holding a clear plastic cup with a lid on it.

I stood up to acknowledge him, and he handed me the cup. "Please go to the bathroom. It's the second door on the left, just through these double doors. Fill it up to the line and then bring it back to me and I'll get your blood work done."

When I returned, he was waiting for me and pointed to a chair, indicating for me to sit down. I handed him my urine sample with a paper towel wrapped around it. I hated walking around with a cup of pee for everyone to see. Why didn't they have one of those windows in the bathroom where I could discretely leave it?

"Tell me your name and date of birth, please."

"Amy Gray-Cunningham and May 13, 1970."

"Which arm would you like me to use?"

"You'll probably like the right arm. Others have told me the vein is perfect and doesn't roll much." Blushing, I smiled up at him, hoping to impress him with my limited knowledge of drawing blood.

He grinned broadly and turned my arm slightly to the left, so he could see. "Yup, you're right, nice vein. "This won't take long.

We have five vials to fill and then you'll be all done." He put a long rubber band around the top of my arm and told me to make a fist. "Small pinch."

I hated the sight of blood, especially my blood, so I looked away. "You want to donate a kidney. Such an amazing gift to give someone. Is it a family member?"

I didn't want to go into the details of not knowing David, so I said, "No, just a friend."

"He must be a great friend for you to go through all of this."

"Yes, I guess so," I replied.

Then he said he was done, and I turned in surprise. "I didn't even feel the needle go in!"

He smiled with a sheepish grin. "Good. It's what I like to hear. You should get the results back in a few days. Your transplant coordinator will give you a call."

He applied a piece of folded gauze with a terry strip tape over it and told me to leave it on for about an hour to minimize bruising.

I said thank you and headed toward the front doors. I prayed, *"Okay Papa, I did my part. Granted, I almost left, but now it's up to You. Give me strength and courage. I love You!"*

CHAPTER TEN

"It is the Spirit who gives life." —John 6:63

"ARE YOU DRESSED IN THE gown yet?" asked my nurse, Beth, as she peered around the curtain into the holding area.

"Yes," I replied and pulled the thin blanket up under my chin, my entire body shaking from the chilly air. Beth reached into a cabinet, grabbed another blanket, and gently laid it on me.

"There, now this should help," she said patting my arm. "I need to get your vitals. Another nurse will be in shortly to start an IV. Do you have any family waiting?"

"Yes. My husband, his parents, and my parents. Do you know where David Ensley is? I'd like to see him before the surgery starts."

"Umm...I'll check and see." She motioned for me to open my mouth and placed the thermometer under my tongue. Then, grabbing my wrist with her two fingers, she glanced at her watch and quietly counted the pulses.

The thermometer beeped, and she removed it. "Good. Temperature is normal. Your vitals look good." Her hands fluttered over the keyboard as she entered the information into my electronic chart. "You rest here while I get your family. I can only allow two people at a time in here. Does it matter who comes back?"

"My husband and mother, please."

"Okay. I'll be back shortly." She pulled open the curtain beside me, and my heart leapt at seeing David lying in the gurney next to me. A smile I couldn't contain spread across my face as I reached out for him. His hand found mine, and our fingers laced together.

"Fancy meeting you here," he said, offering a faint smile.

My pulse quickened. "Yeah, I hear the food's amazing." We both smirked, and our eyes locked. I felt an intimacy between us now which several of weeks ago didn't exist. My heart filled with joy, and I silently thanked God for this miracle.

In a few short hours, my kidney will give life back to David, restoring his ashen gray coloring to a healthy, vibrant pink and his gaunt facial features to a full, robust round, similar to his healthier days. Finally, his body, able to flush the poison which had been killing him for so long, will begin to heal, and his life will be renewed.

I reminisced about when I first met David in early May, at a Mexican restaurant, where we celebrated his mother's birthday. Nervous, I couldn't decide what to wear. What do you wear to meet the person to whom you plan to give your kidney? I searched online but couldn't find fashion etiquette rules helping to provide insight into my dilemma.

Finally, I decided on tan shorts, a white button-down blouse with the sleeves rolled up, sandals and, of course, perfectly polished toes. No proper southern woman would wear sandals without a pedicure.

As Chuck and I turned into the parking lot, I noticed a group of people walking into the restaurant. "Is it them?" I asked, pointing to the front door.

"No, I don't think so. It's been twenty years since I saw them last. But hopefully, they haven't changed much."

Chuck pulled the car in next to a shade tree and popped his lighter to life, as he took a long drag on the cigarette. I hated that he smoked, but over the years I had learned to accept it. I turned away, pretending not to care, and then scanned the parking lot for someone I didn't know.

The temperature felt mild for late spring, but at least it wasn't raining. I breathed in the cool afternoon air. The smell of smoky Mexican fajitas wafted by in the breeze.

My stomach was gripped with anxiety. Feeling light-headed, I inhaled deeply to calm my nerves. I continued breathing deeply for a few moments, hoping my body wouldn't betray me and send me to the bathroom for the rest of the evening. Talk about a great first impression. I thought of David. Is he nervous, too?

Then, from between two parked cars, a burly, fiftyish, fair-skinned man grabbed my husband, lifting him off his feet in a giant bear hug. "Chuck Cunningham! Man, it's good to see you."

"Randy Ensley! Hey man, it's good to see you, too." Chuck managed to break free and turned toward me. "This is my wife, Amy." Randy immediately picked me up in the same giant bear hug, saying, "No introductions...this is our angel!"

As my feet left the ground, I grabbed his shoulder for balance. Standing behind Randy stood a woman with short salt and pepper hair. She gently patted her forehead as beads of perspiration rolled down her face. Still high in the air, I stuck out my hand and said, "Hi, I'm Amy."

"Nice to meet you. I'm Sabra Ensley, Randy's wife." She grabbed his arm, "Put her down."

My feet landed gently back on the pavement. Sabra continued, "David should be here. He's probably inside. Jennifer's on her way with Betty, their mother, and should be here any minute."

Randy started the introductions. First was Katie, their daughter and then, their thirteen-year-old son, Mitchell. Randy and Chuck immediately started reminiscing about the old days at the race track. Randy had helped Chuck get a job at Charlotte Motor Speedway as a security guard back in high school. I wasn't thrilled about the job because he was away on my birthday, but Chuck loved those days and it appeared, so did Randy.

I turned my attention to Sabra, when a thick, southern female voice yelled, "Chuckles!" The vivacious blonde woman, who looked to be in her early forties, wrapped her arms around my husband and said, "I can't believe it's you." Chuck, sensing my glare, gave me a sideways glance, and said, "Jennifer, let me introduce you to my wife, Amy."

She turned around, arms outstretched, and cried out, "Amy-Angel! You're beautiful! It is so good to meet you finally." Tears welled up in her eyes. "Come here, Mama. Meet Amy." Jennifer ushered her over and Betty pulled me into a loving embrace.

"I'm so glad to meet you, Amy. You're the best birthday present ever. You're going to save my son!" She let me go but cradled my face with her hands, "Thank you!" My face flushed as her words overwhelmed me. I didn't know how to respond to all the attention.

"Where's David?" Jennifer asked looking around curiously.

"I'm right here," he said, exiting the restaurant. "I got us a table."

Jennifer grabbed him around his waist and walked him over to me, "Meet Amy-Angel." Our eyes met, and our souls immediately connected. Any lingering doubts evaporated with one look, and I knew my world had shifted forever. Seeing David before me, I knew helping him was more than something I felt "called to do." A tidal wave of conviction flooded my heart and now it was my purpose.

We held each other's gaze for a second more, and then he enveloped me in his arms. "I don't know what to say. I'm so happy to meet you." His eyes moistened with tears, and I wondered what he must be feeling. I was offering him a second chance at life—someone he didn't know. How does a person respond to a gift such as this? Does he dare to dream or hope? What would happen if the kidney donation didn't work? Would he survive? I wondered if these questions haunted him, too?

David wore plain blue jeans and a polo shirt which hung off his tall, lean frame. His shoulders curled forward as if a heavy weight was pressing on them. His face grimaced in pain as he supported himself on a walking cane. Deep wrinkles bracketed his mouth, but his eyes sparkled as a smile danced across his face.

Behind David stood a shy, hesitant woman with a waterfall of blonde hair blown as straight as glass. The light in her eyes appeared faded as if the years of worry and fear had taken their toll. But her soul radiated beauty with a glow of angelic white.

"Meet my wife, Susanne. Susanne, meet Amy." David moved to allow Susanne and me to embrace.

I worried about Susanne's feelings towards me. Would she perceive me as a threat or feel jealous of me? My fears, however, proved unfounded. A pillar of grace, Susanne welcomed me into her family with a warm hug making me feel immediately comfortable. There was a hopefulness in her ocean-blue eyes, calming any reservations I had about her towards me.

Behind Susanne's eyes, however, I could perceive a quiet sadness. The years of hardship over her husband's illness had caused tremendous suffering for her. I silently prayed, *"Papa, I ask for Susanne's eyes to one day sparkle with joy and happiness. Please bless her and heal her heart."*

Wrapping up the introductions, we went inside for dinner. The evening slid by in a blur. Peals of laughter tumbled from our table—especially when a loud drum roll and a clang of symbols filled the restaurant and about ten Mexican waiters gathered around Betty, singing "Happy Birthday" in their best English accents.

A tiny man placed a cake with candles which lit up the room in front of her and placed a huge sombrero on her head, causing the rest of us to roar with excitement. Her face flushed with embarrassment, but Betty cheerfully indulged her swarm of "serenaders" by blowing kisses and shouts of gratitude for their performance.

Standing up, she handed the sombrero back to the little man and said, "Thank you all for the birthday wishes. I'm a very lucky lady. I have my family here to celebrate with me, including my new extended family, Chuck, and Amy and their two boys." She paused, stumbling over her words, but then looked up and stared directly at me, "Soon, Amy will give my son back his life, and there are no words to express my gratitude. Thank you for giving this old woman the best birthday present I could ever wish for." Betty then leaned over and blew out the cluster of candles.

A deafening hoopla resounded throughout the restaurant. Strangers cheered, even though they had no idea what they were celebrating, other than wishing Betty a happy birthday.

"I hope she's right, and I don't let them down." I thought but I didn't say it out loud.

CHAPTER ELEVEN

"A mother's love is everything, Jared. It is what brings a child into this world. It is what molds their entire being. When a mother sees her child in danger, she is literally capable of anything. Mothers have lifted cars off of their children, and destroyed entire dynasties. A mother's love is the strongest energy known to man. You must that love, and its power."
—Jamie McGuire (Eden)

"*NOW, ISN'T THIS JUST COTTON-CANDY-FABULOUS!* You're both right beside each other. Love it. Thank you, Jesus!" She screeched with her hands overhead as if she were in a revival tent meeting.

"I thought only two people were allowed back in pre-op at a time?" I snickered as I sat up a little on my elbows to greet everyone. My mom and step-dad, Chuck, and his parents, Fran and the entire Ensley family gathered around our holding area.

"Just let them try to kick us out of here," Jennifer retorted, flinging up her arms up and landing them on her hips. "I don't think so."

Mom leaned in and kissed my forehead. "Well, the nurse told us only two could come back at a time but didn't say anything as everyone got up to follow her. If they want us out, they'll let us know. How are you feeling?"

"Good. They got the IV started a few minutes ago, and now I'm waiting to see the doctor and the anesthesiologist. They should be by shortly. As far as I know, the surgery is still on schedule."

Mom sat down in the chair beside me and reached out for my hand and gently stroked the top. "Are you sure you're okay?"

"Yes, Mom, I'm good." I replied, trying to reassure her. Besides Chuck, my mom had been my biggest cheerleader. At first, she hated the idea of me donating a kidney to David. I was her child, and she worried about me and the impact of the surgery on my life. I knew everything would work out according to God's plan but making my mom understand it was a different story.

On Mother's Day, we had invited both sides of our family over for a cookout of hamburgers and hotdogs. I enjoyed it when we all got together to celebrate. Chuck and I had decided it would be a good time to tell the family about the donation. I'd been approved pending the results of the MRI scan. We had told David and his family the week before, and only our families were left to inform. The plan was to tell everyone together after dinner; unfortunately, it didn't happen as planned.

My parents and my aunt and uncle were the first to arrive. I poured them each glass of wine and then accompanied them to the patio, while we waited for the rest of the family to get there.

It was a cloudless spring day, and the cool, gentle breeze created a comfortable atmosphere for a cookout. The smell of charcoal pierced the air. Days like this reminded me of why I enjoyed living in the South—it was perfect.

The conversation started off with light talk, as we caught up with work and family and friends. I knew I should've waited for everyone else, including Chuck, but from out of nowhere I blurted out, "I have some exciting news to share with you."

Mom sipped her wine and said with a smile, "I can't wait to hear."

I swallowed the pulsating lump in my throat and pulled in air. How would they take the news and why was I doing this without Chuck? We had a plan but as usual my mouth was getting me into trouble. I proceeded to tell them about the Ensley's and how Chuck knew them from high school. I told them about Jennifer's Facebook page and how David was in renal failure and needed a new kidney. I looked at my mom and saw fear flooding her eyes in anticipation of my news.

"About two months ago, I decided to get tested to be David's donor, and as it turned out, I'm a perfect match for him. The next step is an MRI scan to determine which kidney to use, and then the transplant team will decide if I'm approved. Afterward, they'll schedule the surgery."

Tears welled up in my mother's eyes, and she mouthed my words as I spoke as if she were trying to make sense of what she heard. Then she murmured, "No, no, no," and wagged her finger gently from left to the right trying to comprehend what I just told her. "Please tell me you're not planning to do this?"

"Yes, Mom, I am. I know it's a shock and probably the last thing you thought you'd hear from me, but I'm doing this. I feel God has called me, and I'm following His direction in my life. It's not something I've entered into lightly, either. Chuck and I have discussed it, and I've prayed about it; heck, I've even tried to talk myself out if it. But miracles are happening, and I can't believe I'm allowed to be a part of them."

Chuck opened the sliding glass door and immediately knew what I had done by the thickness in the air. He looked at me and asked, "Did you...?"

"Yes," I interrupted him. "I told them, and I know I should've waited for you, but the timing seemed perfect, so I went for it."

Uncle Don stood up and said, "Well, personally I think it's awesome!"

"Thank you, Uncle Don. I agree with you. It is awesome and last few months have been amazing." I replied.

"Well, I don't think it's awesome. Not one bit." My mother

shot up from the table and bolted into the house. My step-father got up to follow her, and I jumped up, "Let me, Terry, this is between her and me."

Entering the house, I saw her closing the front door. She was upset, and I kicked myself for not sticking with the plan and waiting for Chuck. But I knew either way it wouldn't have mattered. Mom would've had a hard time with the news anyway because I was her daughter and her first instinct was to protect me. I knew she thought I was intentionally putting myself in harm's way with an unnecessary surgery. I prayed God would help her see that He had it all under control.

"Mom," I said as I opened the front door. "Mom, will you talk to me?"

"What do you want me to say to you? I understand? I agree with what you're doing? You're having major surgery, and anything can happen. Do you understand there is a possibility you could die? Do you?"

"Yes, Mom. I'm not blind to the fact there are complications with any surgery. But I believe in the depths of my soul God will take care of me. I believe there is a higher purpose here, and, Mom, He's asked me to save a person's life. David has a wife and two daughters. What about them, Mom? His girls deserve to have their dad walk them down the aisle and dance with them on their wedding day. His wife deserves to grow old with her best friend, and Mom, I have the power to make it all happen. God has given me the perfect kidney. How can I say no?"

We stared at each other with tears rolling down our cheeks. Mom pulled me into her arms. "I love you, Amy. You're my daughter and I deserve to have you in my life. But I'll be there with you every step of the way. If you change your mind it's okay. You don't have to save the world."

"I'm not trying to save the world—only one man."

CHAPTER TWELVE

" 'Thank you' is the best prayer that anyone could say. I say that one a lot. Thank you expresses extreme gratitude, humility, understanding." —Alice Walker

CONVERSATIONS IN THE PRE-OP ROOM flowed around me as if I were a rock in a stream. I watched with delight as my family's excitement and energy permeated the air. The noise level rose steadily, and I was afraid we'd get in trouble for having too many people around, but the nurses didn't say a word. Suddenly, Dr. Peterson and another doctor appeared in front of me and with a deep sigh he pulled the curtain around my gurney closed.

Dressed in greenish-blue surgical scrubs, Dr. Peterson looked even more striking and rugged than when I first met him at my initial screening appointment. His wavy brown hair was visible just below the cap on his head, and the light stubble on his face gave the impression he'd been at the hospital for a while even though it was still early.

Smiling placidly at me from the foot of my gurney, he said, "Hi, Amy. How are you feeling this morning? It looks as if you have a considerable following." He smirked and turned to introduce himself to my family. "Hello, my name is Dr. Peterson. I'm the surgeon performing Amy's part of the surgery today."

Chuck reached to shake his hand, "Hello, Dr. Peterson. We met a while back. I'm Amy's husband, Chuck, and this is her mother and stepfather, Linda and Terry, my sister Fran, and my parents, Charles and Joyce."

"Oh, yes, of course. It's good to see you again, Chuck." Dr. Peterson replied.

Feeling the need to defend the amount of people congregating in his pre-op room, I explained, "Just so you're aware, the nurses know everyone is here, but if I need to ask them to leave, I will."

"No problem, Amy. It's good to see so many people here to support you. I love it. Besides, we're almost ready to take you back. So, they'll have to leave. Do you have any questions for me?"

"No, not right now. I'm just ready to get started." I said, feeling butterflies fluttering in my stomach.

"I'm sure you are," he replied and gently patted my knee. Then he turned to Chuck and my mother and asked, "How about you two? Any questions?"

"How long will the surgery take?" Chuck asked.

"Good question. About four hours total, but Amy's part, maybe about two. We'll take her back first and get her prepped and ready. Then the recipient's surgical team will do the same with him. He'll be in the adjacent operating room, and once he's ready, we'll remove Amy's kidney and hand it off to them. We won't remove it until he's ready and his team gives me the go ahead. Then we'll close her up and take her down to recovery. But you won't be able to see her until she gets into her room. So, it'll probably be three to four hours once the surgery begins. Also, I'll send someone out to give you periodical updates on the procedure; you'll know exactly how it's progressing."

We all looked at him wide-eyed nodding in agreement.

"Just make sure everything goes back in where it belongs and don't leave anything in that is not supposed to be there like a sponge or knife. Okay?" I said, jokingly.

Dr. Peterson chuckled, "I think I can handle it. Now don't worry—you're in good hands." He patted my knee again and turned to shake Chuck's hand and then my mother's.

He looked back at me and winked, "I'll see you shortly!"

Dr. Peterson stepped out from the curtain and began to pull it closed again when Jennifer grabbed it and said, "It's okay to keep it open. We'd like a moment with Amy to pray together." Then she looked at me, "if it's okay with you?"

"Sounds like a great idea. Thank you, Jennifer!"

I reached out and found David's thin, battered hand and gave it a gentle squeeze. About twenty people gathered around David and me, holding hands and bowing their heads in silence as Reverend Toomey, from Jennifer's church, began to pray.

Once again, I wondered if David was scared or anxious. This whole experience must have been unbelievable for him. One minute he was preparing to die and living with the knowledge he would leave his family. Then, the next minute, we're in the hospital as we prepared for the doctors to heal his failing body with my kidney. What a miracle I had the privilege to participate in.

Twenty years ago, however, I couldn't say this would have been possible—although I do believe God was working to manifest this miracle even then.

At seventeen, I was addicted to cocaine. I lived for myself and the constant search for the next high. I didn't believe in a God, or at least in the knowledge of a God who loved me. But I always craved His unconditional love and thought I had found a sense of security and belonging in a needle. Somewhere along the way, my love for cocaine turned on me, and I became its loyal and subjective servant. Whatever it asked, I did, because I needed the next high.

I stole checks and cashed them for money to pay for my next fix. Life revolved around getting and staying high. I loved the chase just as much as the high.

Eventually, my lying and stealing caught up with me and I was wanted on felony fraud charges. Scared, I turned to my mother. I have no idea how she did it or to whom she talked, but I never spent a day in jail—"but for the grace of God I go." He afforded me mercy because I definitely didn't get what I deserved.

It felt like someone else living my life back then. I would scarcely know that girl now. But, I wouldn't change anything about those experiences. I firmly believe that in order to appreciate and live in the light, you have to entertain the shadows.

Back in the hospital room, tears of gratitude filled my eyes. The preacher began, "Father, we thank you for Your mercy and grace. We thank you for Amy and her family. She's so unselfishly given of herself and her body to save the life of one of Your beloved children. We ask You now to send your Holy Spirit to guide the hands of the doctors and nurses. We ask for Your Spirit to fill the operating room and for Your presence to flood us all. Thank You for saving David's life. His wife, his children, and his family and friends thank you. We ask You to provide peace and comfort to Amy's husband, Chuck and her family as she heads into surgery. You have heard our prayers and have faithfully answered them. To You be all the honor and glory. Amen." And another Amen was heard in unison.

I looked over at David and his crooked smile lit up his face. He mouthed the words, "thank you," and I responded, mouthing, "You're welcome."

David had lost about forty pounds and resembled an Ethiopian famine victim. His ashy-gray skin draped over his bones like a blanket, and his eyes, dull and lifeless, sunk into his skull. But there was a twinkle—a glimmer of hope, which glistened in his eyes which a few weeks ago didn't exist.

I murmured, *"Papa, thank You for this miracle. Thank You for allowing me to be a part of it. I ask Your Spirit to breathe life into my kidney as they place it in David's body. I ask it to start working immediately, giving him life and good health."*

Everyone kissed and hugged after Reverend Toomey lifted us up in prayer. The room was filled with light and love, and I knew something good was happening; I felt it in my soul.

The surgery posed possible complications for both David and me. Also, David's body could reject the kidney, even though we were a close match. But I knew in every part of my being God was in charge, and I had never felt His presence as strongly as I did in that moment. We were all witnessing a miracle.

CHAPTER THIRTEEN

"Being deeply loved by someone gives you strength, while loving someone deeply gives you courage."
—Lao Tzu

SUDDENLY, DAVID'S NURSE EMERGED FROM the crowd of people and said only immediate family was allowed to stay. Everyone else would need to move to the waiting room. The surgical teams were coming shortly to get us for surgery.

Mom stood up and planted a soft kiss on my cheek. "I love you, sweetheart. Pops and I will go to the waiting room, so Chuck can stay here with you. I'll see you soon." Her warm tears softly fell on my cheek, and I replied, "I love you too, Mom. I'll see you in a few hours." She turned to meet my stepfather's arm as he reached out to help her walk.

"We'll see you soon, Amy," Pops said, blowing me a kiss before moving towards the exit door with my mother.

I hugged Fran, Granna, and PopPop as they left for the waiting room. "I'm praying for you," Granna mumbled.

"Thank you, Granna. I love you all!"

Jennifer, sobbing, came over and kissed me on my cheek. "Thank you, Amy-Angel. We all adore you!"

"Same here. It'll be okay. David and I have this—we'll see you after the surgery."

Betty reached around Jennifer and grabbed my hand. But she didn't say anything—she didn't have too. Her face said it all.

After everyone had left, Chuck sat down beside me in the chair Mom had been sitting in and reached for my hand. Fear and worry was stretched across his face; I tried to comfort him. "Honey, it'll be okay."

"No, it won't be, not until you're out of surgery and safe. Don't try to tell me otherwise."

We both looked up as the anesthesiologist stood beside my gurney. Like Dr. Peterson, he wore greenish-blue scrubs with a surgical cap on his head. His hair was clean shaven close to the nape of his neck, so it almost appeared as if he had no hair. But having met him at the pre-op appointment, I knew he wore his hair shaved close. He wasn't as good looking as Dr. Peterson but in his own way I knew he was a charmer. I wasn't sure how old he was, but his left hand didn't reveal a ring or a tan line, so I assumed he was young and single.

"Well, we're almost ready for you. But I wanted to go over a few more things with you first."

"Okay," I nodded.

"We will give you a shot in your IV shortly, which will cause you to relax and feel a little drowsy. Then, when we get into the operating room, I'll put a large mask over your face and you'll go to sleep. With the drugs I give you, you should stay asleep throughout the entire surgery."

He remembered my biggest fear. When I had my appendix removed several years before, I woke up in the middle of the surgery. Nothing in life could prepare you for waking up, even briefly, to see a doctor holding your guts in his hands.

"Thank you, Dr. Young."

He smiled and continued, "Just to confirm, you're not allergic to any medications?"

"No."

"Perfect, and then I'll send your nurse to give you the shot in the IV. Are there any other questions for me before I go?"

We shook our heads no. Chuck reached out for the doctor's hand and stared him in the eye and said, "Thank you. Take good care of my girl!"

"I will. I promise."

Dr. Young headed off toward the nurse's station, and Chuck turned back to me. "Wow, I can't believe this is happening."

Chuck's eyes moistened, and he looked away briefly, so I wouldn't see.

I grabbed his arm and said, "Chuck, you're my best friend and you've been amazing, and I wouldn't have gotten this far without you. I know this next part will be hard for you but remember God is in charge, and He will see me—us—through it."

"I know your faith is strong, but I don't think I'm as brave as you, Amy. I love you and want you with me always."

"And I will be. You're stronger than you think. You're the strongest man I know." I wished I could alleviate Chuck's fear and anxiety.

Beth came in and said, "I'm sorry to interrupt, but they're almost ready for you, and I need to give you this medicine to help you relax before they take you to surgery. You'll feel drowsy but mostly just relaxed. Are you okay? Do you need any more blankets?"

"No, I'm fine. Thank you though."

"Well, they will be here to get you shortly."

"Thanks."

Just then, I realized the curtain between David and I was pulled closed at some point. I asked Chuck, "When did the curtain get closed? Is David still over there or have they taken him?"

"Nope, I'm still here!"

Laughing, Chuck reached over and pulled the curtain open. David and his wife, Susanne, were smiling widely at us.

David had a glazed expression, as though he had received the same medication I had, and we both had started feeling the effects.

"So, did they give you some of the good stuff, too?" I asked him.

"Yeah, I think I could fly!" he said with his arms stretched out like an airplane.

"No, you don't. You stay in your bed," Susanne scolded.

I was about to respond to him when my escorts arrived to take me to the operating room. "Amy Gray-Cunningham?"

"Yes...ummm...I'm Amy."

The nurse approached my gurney and reached for my arm with the admitting bracelet. "Can you tell me your name again and date of birth?"

I smirked at Chuck and gave her the information she requested.

"Great. Are you ready?"

"I think so." I glanced over at Chuck and I could tell he was doing everything possible not to lose it. I smiled, and he smiled back.

Tania, the transplant coordinator assigned to my case, told me I could change my mind right up to the moment they rolled me into surgery. She would tell everyone the doctors canceled the transplant due to a medical reason. I was no longer a viable candidate. But I knew I wouldn't change my mind, although it was comforting knowing there was an option.

"Well, Dr. Peterson is waiting for you in the operating room. What do you say we don't keep him waiting?" The nurse said as she went around to the back of my gurney and stepped on a couple of peddles to release the brakes.

"Let's do it," I replied. I touched David's hand briefly and said, "Next time we meet, you'll be dancing."

"I promise. Thank you, Amy." he said. Susanne stood beside him with tears streaming down her cheeks. I waved as the nurse pushed me towards the exit door.

Chuck took my hand as he walked with us. Once we got to the double doors, the other nurse punched the silver pad on the wall and said, "You'll have to say your good-byes here. This is as far as you can go, Mr. Cunningham."

Chuck nodded and bent down to kiss me. "You're my heart—remember always."

"You're mine, too, and I'll see you when I wake up."

Then the nurse guided the gurney into the hallway, and I turned slightly backward to see Chuck as the large double doors closed in front of him.

PART TWO

CHAPTER FOURTEEN

"Part of me suspects I'm a loser, and part of me thinks I'm God Almighty." — John Lennon

THE FLUORESCENT LIGHTS SLID BY in a blur as a nurse rolled me down the hallway. I heard a faint murmur of someone asking a question, but I couldn't make it out. The voice sounded muddled as if I were under water.

Then, Dr. Peterson appeared in front of me, "Amy, you're in the surgery room now. Go to sleep and I'll see you when you wake up. You're in good hands. I've got you."

"Okay," I managed in a groggy voice.

I had liked Dr. Peterson from the moment I first time met him because Chuck's entire attitude about the surgery had changed after meeting him. I'm not sure exactly what happened, whether it was Chuck finally understanding the transplant process better or Dr. Peterson's manner in general that put him at ease, but it didn't matter. I was grateful for the change in Chuck's mood and demeanor.

A few weeks before the appointment with Dr. Peterson, Chuck and I had a major fight about my decision to donate a kidney while at a restaurant. I had received a call from Tania, the transplant coordinator, informing me the initial blood work and urine tests had come back showing David and I were a compatible match. She wanted to know if I would like to proceed with the next step and meet with her and the transplant team. I told Chuck about the call over dinner.

"What exactly does a 'negative cross-match' mean?" Chuck snapped.

"It means David's blood doesn't have any antibodies which would reject my DNA, so he'll most likely accept the transplant."

Tania had explained the results to me in detail, which helped me interpret them for Chuck. I could tell by his rising voice that my detailed information didn't interest him too much.

My heartbeat quickened, and I proceeded cautiously. "Based on the tissue typing, David and I are a 3, which means we could've been siblings."

Chuck looked at me with a raised eyebrow, and as his mouth

filled with words to refute my last sentence, I quickly continued, hoping to make him understand. "We're all born with six different tissue antigens—three from each parent. On a scale of 0-to-6, with 6 a perfect match being identical twins and 0 unrelated, we're a 3. Siblings have a 50-percent chance of being a 3. Isn't this amazing, Chuck? Who would've thought I would be such a close match to a stranger? Do you know what this means for a successful transplant for David?"

"You're worried about a stranger's chances of survival? What about me? What about the boys? What happens to us if you die? And don't start with the statistics again. I don't want to hear it. There's still a chance something will go wrong, and I don't care how slim you say it might be—it's still there and could very well happen!"

By this time, people in the restaurant tried politely not to stare by averting their eyes, but regardless, heads turned our way as Chuck's voice rose. "I can't believe you are willing to put your life—our family—at risk for someone you don't even know all because you heard a voice telling you to do it! Do you know how ridiculous you sound?"

Immediately, I regretted spilling my secret to him. I knew he wouldn't understand. And now total strangers didn't understand, either.

His words, razor sharp, sliced through me. "Chuck, will you keep your voice down, please?"

Slamming his fork down on the table, he replied, "I'm done.

I'll meet you in the car." And he stormed out of the restaurant without even glancing back, leaving me in disbelief.

A mixture of guilt and anger rose in me as I felt the blood creeping up the back of my neck and flowing into my cheeks. I motioned for the waiter, "Can I have the check, please?"

CHAPTER FIFTEEN

"If you save one life, it is as though you saved the world." —The Talmud

IT TOOK A COUPLE OF weeks to schedule the next meeting because Tania wanted me to meet with the entire transplant team in one day. Thankfully, Chuck agreed to go with me, and we both took the day off from work.

First, we would meet with her at 8 in the morning for about 30 minutes, and then take a series of X-rays and a CT scan. After lunch, we would meet with the nutritionist, financial advisor, social worker and then finally the nephrologist or kidney doctor. They all played a role in deciding whether to approve me as a donor.

We arrived about 7:50a.m., and as we walked in, I saw Chuck's shoulders tense up. I knew he wasn't happy about this, but I also knew he wouldn't dream of telling me not to go through with it. He may not have liked it, but he loved and supported me regardless. And I loved him even more for it, especially since I knew how much this cost him emotionally.

I checked in with the receptionist while Chuck found us seats along the back-side of the lobby. I watched as he swiped his phone and tapped in his password. Instinctively, I knew he pressed the Candy Crush icon—his favorite game.

The receptionist took my name and told me Tania would be out to meet me shortly. I thanked her and left to take the seat next to my husband. A smile filled my face as I glanced to see him diligently "clearing candies" by combining like-colored candy to clean the board. He was, if nothing else, predictable.

Watching the hands on the wall clock drag from one number to the next, I waited with anticipation for Tania. Although I had spoken to her several times on the phone, I had yet to meet her and wondered what she looked like. *You'll know soon enough,* I told myself. *Be patient.*

Several people, whom I assumed were nurses and patients, walked through the side door. Suddenly, a woman about my height with shoulder-length amber-colored hair stepped through the door and called my name.

My heart skipped and my throat clenched making words impossible to find. Standing up to meet her, I whispered, "I'm Amy."

She walked over and offered me her hand. "Hi, I'm Tania Summers. It's a pleasure to meet you finally."

"Same here." I turned and introduced Chuck.

"It's good to meet you, too. I'm glad you were both able to come. One of the things we evaluate is the donor's support system. So, the fact that you're here is a good thing."

Chuck rolled a doubtful look my way but didn't say a word.

"Well, shall we get started?" We followed Tania through the side door. She stopped at the nurses' station and handed me a small plastic cup.

"Amy, would you mind giving me another urine sample? The bathrooms are right over there," she said pointing in the direction of two big brown doors.

I took the container and did as instructed. When I came out, Tania took my specimen wrapped in a paper towel and placed the cup in the tray on the counter. "I'll get someone to take care of it in a moment. Please stand on the scale so I can get your weight. How tall are you?"

"Five feet, two and a half inches," I replied as I slipped off my sandals before stepping on the scale. *Every ounce counts*, I thought.

"Perfect– 144 pounds. Good." She motioned for me to follow her as she moved into a small room to the right of the nurse's station.

The room was small, almost like an oversized closet. To the

left, stood an examination table with two blue-vinyl upholstered chairs positioned on each end. Sunlight slanted in through the metal blinds in the two square windows above the chairs. Chuck glanced up from his phone and quietly pressed a button to turn it off as I settled into the seat beside him.

Tania grabbed the rolling stool and sat in front of us. Placing the folders she held on the counter next to her, she threaded her fingers together and placed them in her lap.

Smiling at us, she began, "I'm glad you're here. I'm sure you have plenty of questions for me, but first I need to ask you if you have been threatened, coerced in any way, or promised monetary compensation for donating your kidney?"

"Absolutely not," I replied. Chuck's jaw dropped but she had asked me this before, so I wasn't shocked.

"Good. Legally, I have to ask because if someone is threatening you to make this decision or promised money, it's illegal and we couldn't proceed any further. Also, I want you to understand you are in no way obligated to go through with the donation. If anytime you wish to stop, just tell me and I'll tell whomever you weren't approved. Do you understand?"

"Yes."

"Good. I'll ask you this almost every time we meet. I want to make sure you know you're under no obligation to proceed. Since this is an elective surgery for you, I need you to be aware of your rights."

"I understand. But I want to do this. I'm not being coerced or threatened, and I have not received any money. Heck, we haven't even told David, yet."

Tania nodded and asked Chuck, "And what about you, Mr. Cunningham? How do you feel about all this?"

"Chuck. Please, call me Chuck. To be honest with you, I'm not crazy about the idea, but Amy has her mind set on this. I'm here to learn more about the surgery and what it means for her. I admire her for wanting to help David, but I'm also worried about her health and any long-term complications she would experience from having only one kidney."

"Thank you for your honesty, Chuck. Most spouses express the same worries and concerns when they come in here. Being a living donor is a major life-changing experience and something you shouldn't enter into lightly. It's why we have you meeting with so many people today. We want you to know everything about the surgery—what it'll mean for you both financially, medically, emotionally, and spiritually. Not only do we need to make sure you, Amy, are physically healthy enough to be a donor but also understand your emotional, spiritual and financial health is important to us."

Chuck and I bobbed our heads in agreement.

"Good. Now, Amy, I'm sure you've done a great deal of research about kidney disease and transplant but I'm going to give you more information. Stop me if you have any questions. Okay?"

"Yes," Chuck and I said in unison.

"Here at CMC, we have been doing kidney transplants since 1970, and on August 8, 1971, we performed our first living kidney donation. We are a leading center for kidney transplants and one of the busiest renal transplant centers in the nation, which means we do this a lot. To date, we've done over 2,600 successful surgeries and also to date we have not lost a donor or a recipient as a result of a transplant."

"Well, let's make sure I'm not the first, okay?" I said jokingly.

"I sure hope not. But it brings up a good point. As I mentioned, this is an elective surgery for you, and with any surgery there are risks. Now, we have been successful in minimizing those risks, but we can't control them all. As I said, however, we take every precaution to protect the donor, and it's why we've been so fortunate."

"Good to know," I replied. Her words seemed to hang in the air as Chuck drew in a slow deliberate breath.

"When we first started performing transplants, it was very hard on the donors. We would cut the patient from stem-to-sternum, making an incision from the belly button to the middle of the back." Tania showed us by moving her hand from the middle of her stomach around to the middle of her back.

"Today, we do a laparoscopic procedure in which the surgeons make three tiny incisions—one from the belly button down to the top of the bikini line, another small one on the right side of the abdomen, and the third on the left. This procedure is less invasive for the donor and requires less recovery time. But the surgeon will explain it more when you see him." She looked through the chart on the counter.

"It looks like you'll see Dr. Peterson this afternoon at 3 p.m. You'll like him. He's young but he is one of our leading renal transplant surgeons."

"Will he also be David's doctor?" asked Chuck.

"No, both Amy and David will have a separate transplant team which consists of a nephrologist/surgeon, surgical nurse, psychologist, nutritionist, financial advisor, and then, of course, me—the coordinator. I'm your advocate for everything—kind of like the gatekeeper. Nobody gets to you except through me. So, if you ever have any questions or concerns, or if a member of our staff treats you unfairly, let me know, and I'll take care of it."

"Great, thank you," I said.

"Okay, so your next appointment is with X-ray." Glancing at her watch, she continued, "You'll need to get going to make it on time. Do you know where it is?"

"Yes, we have the map you emailed me. We should be fine."

I gathered my purse and water bottle and then, rose to shake Tania's extended hand.

"Thank you," I said.

"No problem. Make sure to write down any questions you

think of today. We'll meet again this afternoon before you leave and discuss your questions then. Good luck."

Tania escorted us back to the lobby. Chuck extended his arm to open the front door and sunlight poured into the dimly lit lobby. Then he shrugged and said, "Well, here we go. For better or worse, right?"

"Right," I replied and reached out for his arm. "For better or worse. I love you, and I couldn't do this without you."

"And you won't ever have to. Now let's get you to X-ray—if we can find it. I hope you understand how to read this map because I sure don't."

Unfolding the map, he moved toward the parking lot. Then, glancing over his shoulder back at me, he said, "Well, are you coming?"

CHAPTER SIXTEEN

"To the world you may be one person, but to one person, you may be the world." — Dr. Seuss

"ALL DONE," I SAID TO Chuck as I came through the door. "Let's get something to eat. I'm starving."

"Okay, how did it go?"

"Not bad. The EKG technician was a little weird at first, but she said my heart was perfect and to give this to Tania." I held up the long sheet of wiggly lines indicating my heart was healthy and normal.

As we left the waiting room and padded down the long corridor towards the cafeteria, I continued talking about the chunky, middle-aged EKG technician who wasn't very friendly. She came across as an insecure, anxiety-ridden person whose sole purpose in life was to make other people miserable. But after I told her about wanting to be a living kidney donor, her mood lifted, and a sweet smile eased across her face, opening the door to an interesting conversation. By the time I left, we were talking about her children and her dreams of one day becoming a doctor.

"Her transformation was inspiring," I said to Chuck. "I'm glad she softened up. She's an intelligent, funny lady who just happened to have had a bad morning."

"You're weird!" Chuck said jokingly, poking me in the side.

"I know, but you have to love me anyway," I said as I planted a noisy kiss on his cheek.

"Okay, if you say so. What do you want to eat? Salad or sandwich?" Chuck asked as he pointed to the enormous salad bar in the middle of the cafeteria.

"I'm not sure. I'm going to look around, and I'll meet you at the check-out counter."

Threading a path through the crowd, I looked over the options and eventually decided on a chicken salad wrap, fruit, and water. Chuck and I laughed when we met up because we ended up with the same lunch, except no fruit for him.

Locating a table in the corner, we made our way through the maze of people. "We have an hour before we meet with the social worker back at the transplant clinic, so take your time," I said.

Chuck grabbed his phone out of his pocket and touched the icon to open the Candy Crush game. I smiled over at him, and he asked, "What?"

"Nothing, nothing. Play your game. I can read my book." We

both settled in to eat but reading proved difficult as images of the morning continued to flash by in my mind.

The X-ray went quickly, and we didn't have trouble finding it, though Chuck worried about it. It was just as the directions indicated—5th floor and the second door on the left off the elevators. The small waiting room consisted of two metal folding chairs and a dimly lit lamp on a rickety, old brown table. We were the only people there, and I was in and out in a matter of minutes.

The EKG appointment, however, took forever. My appointment was at 10:30 a.m. and because the X-ray finished early, we sat in the waiting room from 10a.m. until almost an hour later when Sylvia, the EKG technician, came to get me.

At least, the chairs were more comfortable than in the X-ray waiting room. The rectangular room opened up to a long corridor leading to the heart unit. Now and then, people in green scrubs and white coats flew by headlong toward the double doors at the end of the hallway, making me a little nervous and uncomfortable.

I prayed God would help whomever it was they were racing toward. *"Papa, give the doctors hands to heal and the wisdom to know what to do and let them get there quickly."*

"Amy, are you ready? We should get going, or we'll be late for your next appointment," Chuck said, breaking into my thoughts.

My gaze came back into focus, and I nodded blearily, "Yeah, I'm ready."

Chuck slipped in beside me, stretching an arm around my waist, "Where did you go there? You looked lost in thought."

"Oh, nowhere. I was just thinking about this morning and hoping all goes well," I said with a reassuring smile. I thought it best not to tell him my thoughts about the people the doctors hurried to save earlier.

CHAPTER SEVENTEEN

"Everything that is not given is lost." — Mother Teresa

WE ARRIVED BACK AT THE clinic a few minutes before my scheduled appointment with the social worker. After checking in with the receptionist, I took a seat beside Chuck.

Glancing over his arm at his phone, I asked, "What are you playing now? No Candy Crush?"

"What are you doing, spying on me?" he asked, as his lips spread into a playful smile.

"No, I just want to know what you're playing. I can't believe it's not Candy Crush."

"It's Bubble Witch Saga if you must know, Ms. Busybody," drawing out each syllable.

"Is it fun?"

"Would I be playing it if it wasn't? And don't go copying me either. You always have to copy me."

"I'll copy you if I want to. It's in the marriage contract you signed right under the wife can do whatever she wants and is always right."

"Oh yeah, I don't remember signing it."

Then I heard my name called for the fourth time today. I looked up and saw a slender, petite woman with a beautiful oval face and a neat blonde ponytail holding a clipboard.

Chuck and I made our way to her, and she broke into a grin, grabbed my hand and began pumping it.

"My name is Beth McCoy. It's nice to meet you."

"And you, too," I replied.

She held the door open, and we slipped past her as she said, "Follow me. We're going to an office down the hallway on the corner."

As instructed, we followed her into a tiny room. A large, empty bookcase lined the left wall and an oversized round table with four chairs filled up the rest of the room. I took a seat by the window, and Chuck filed in beside me.

"I'm glad you both could come today. I know Tania tries to schedule all the appointments with the transplant team in one day. It can make for a long day sometimes."

"Yes, but we don't mind. I think it's better to do it all at one time," I responded.

"Good. So, tell me a little about yourself, Amy. What made you decide to be a donor?"

I glanced over at Chuck as he shifted uncomfortably in his chair. "Well, it hasn't been an easy decision, but I feel it's what I'm supposed to do—or rather what I'm led to do."

"What do you mean by "supposed to do?" she asked.

"It all started when Chuck told me about a Facebook page a friend of his from high school created, searching for a kidney for her brother. I didn't know a person could donate a kidney while they were still alive. I always thought it was something you did after you died. So, at first, I didn't know what to think about it, but I couldn't get this man or his situation off my mind."

I decided not to tell her I heard God speak directly to me, announcing I would be the one to save David's life. Since she was a social worker, I didn't want to end up in the mental ward, instead of going home tonight. But I continued to tell her about my faith in God and how I felt led to apply to be David's donor.

"I haven't entered into this lightly. I've prayed about it, and Chuck and I have discussed it at length. But to be honest with you, I never thought I'd get this far. Although for me it just confirms what I'm doing is the right thing.

"You say you haven't entered into this lightly—what does it mean exactly? Are you prepared mentally, emotionally and financially for what this may cost you? Have you considered the risk of something happening to your remaining kidney and having to go on dialysis yourself?"

"I've researched living donors, and I know some of what to expect after the surgery. I've also read if anything were to happen to me I would be placed at the top of the transplant list. But I honestly don't think it'll happen and if it does then I'll deal with it then. As I've told Chuck, I can't make my decision based on what-ifs. I can't explain it, but I just know I'm meant to do this. As for the financial issues, Tania's told me David's insurance will pay for everything related to the surgery, and my only responsibility is the time I need to take off from work, which I don't think will be a problem."

"Have you told your boss yet about your plans?" she asked, placing the pen in her hand on the clipboard.

"Oh no, not yet. I thought I'd wait to see if I get approved first."

"You might want to consider finding out if they offer short-term disability because you'll be out of work for at least 6 to 8 weeks. Usually, the insurance company pays 60-40 or at best 70-30. I have seen some companies pay 100 percent, but it's rare. Will you be able to afford a salary cut during your recovery time?"

"Great question! We'll have to discuss it, but I'm sure we can work it out financially for a few weeks." I looked at Chuck. He wasn't saying a word.

"Beth, honestly, I don't know what's going to happen or even what to think about everything. I'm taking it one step at a time. I have no idea why I've been chosen for this miracle or if it'll go anywhere, but all I know is I've felt a deep desire to apply. So here I am."

"What about you, Chuck? How do you feel about all of this?" Beth asked as she rotated the handle on her coffee cup with perfectly manicured nails.

He didn't answer for several beats and then finally said, "I'm here to support Amy. At first, I thought she was crazy for doing this, and I've tried to talk her out of it. But once she decides on something, there's no stopping her. Although I admire her for what she's doing, I admit I'm scared. I don't want to lose her. But her amazing, kind heart is one of the reasons I love her, so I'm here to learn and understand. No matter what, I support Amy and I believe in her. So, if she feels God wants her to do this, then who am I to stop her?"

The drone of the ceiling fan filled my ears as I wiped the moisture from my eyes. How could I be so lucky to have such a wonderful man in my life? What did I do to deserve him?

"Chuck, thank you for sharing your thoughts and being honest. I can understand your hesitancy, but I applaud your courage—both of you. I think you two have a healthy attitude and outlook on the surgery. Do either of you have any questions for me?" Beth asked.

"I don't think I do. Chuck, what about you?" I asked as I gently stroked the top of his hand.

"No, not right now."

"Okay, well, here is my card. If you think of anything, please call me anytime. I'm here to help."

Taking her card, we nodded in agreement. "We will, I promise, and thank you for your time."

We rose from the chairs as Beth reached for the door and turned the knob. Chuck found my hand; our fingers threaded together, and we fell in behind her as she escorted us to the nurses' station to meet Tania for our next appointment with the nutritionist.

CHAPTER EIGHTEEN

"Try to be a rainbow in someone's cloud."
—Maya Angelou

TANIA LED US BACK TO the room we met in earlier. "Have a seat. Belinda will be in to see you shortly."

"Thank you," I replied.

We each settled into the seat we had before, like an old habit rediscovered. I fished into my purse for my phone and entered my passcode. Since we were waiting, I thought I'd check emails before she arrived. Chuck, of course, played the new game he had downloaded. I welcomed the silence between us for the moment. Things had gotten emotional in the meeting with the social worker, and I expected Chuck needed a break. I knew I did.

I realized the day wouldn't be easy, but I had to admit I felt drained. Listening to Chuck made me understand his reluctance but I appreciated him supporting me regardless. It made me wonder if I was doing the right thing. I could easily just get up and walk out. But something kept me from moving as it has before when doubts crept in.

It was hearing God's Voice which kept me still. It was clear and distinct about what would happen, and I believed it. So, I stayed and waited.

A little while later, as I absently twisted the cap on my water bottle, Belinda, the nutritionist, asked me, "So, what did you eat yesterday?"

"Let me start by telling you I don't eat "bad," but it's not always good, either, I guess." I felt the need to assure her I did, for the most part, eat a healthy diet. Although I probably ate more cookies and pizzas than I should, I didn't want her to know it.

Probably just out of college, Belinda, was petite with flawless porcelain skin and ringlets of blonde hair. Her petite size, fitness and attractiveness, made me strangely uncomfortable, sitting in close proximity to her. I think I would've been more relaxed if she hadn't been so perfect looking.

"Okay, good. Now tell me what you ate."

"Well, in the morning I had a bagel, a sandwich and apple for lunch and then spaghetti for dinner."

"Are those typical meals for you and do you drink alcohol?" she asked jotting down notes on her pad.

"Yes, but, of course, I mix it up and, yes, I do like wine with dinner. Also, I feel breakfast is the most important meal, so I always make sure I eat well then, but also, I drink a lot of water," holding up my water bottle.

"Good, good. Excellent," she replied nodding her head at both Chuck and me.

She continued peppering me with questions about my health, my level of exercise and my sleep patterns. Then she explained a healthy diet consisted of fresh fruits and vegetables, plenty of greens and lean meats, such as chicken, fish and turkey. Also, one-to-two servings of grains a day were plenty.

"Your weight seems to be in a suitable range now, but a few more pounds and your BMI would be too high. You'd have to lose weight before being approved for the surgery. Watch your portion sizes. From what you've told me, you're eating healthy, although you need to add more greens to your diet and be careful about your portion sizes. It's just as important as what you eat."

My mouth dropped open, and my eyes widened. Did she just call me fat? Color prickled onto my cheeks, and emotion choked in my throat as I tried to remain calm.

"Yes, thank you. I'll take it into consideration."

My face must have broadcasted my feelings because Belinda followed up by saying, "As I said, your weight is good now but just watch how much you eat. Now, do you have any questions for me?"

"Ah, no, I can't think of anything right now. You've been very helpful," I said, my jaw tightened as I seethed with anger.

She stood and extended a hand. "You're welcome and good luck with everything. It was nice meeting you both."

As she opened the door, light from the hallway trickled in, and when the door closed behind her with a gentle click, I turned to Chuck, "Oh my God— did you hear her? She called me fat!" I said, drawing the words out.

"What are you talking about?" he asked, oblivious to the whole conversation.

"She said my weight was 'suitable,'" I replied, my fingers motioning in an air quote. "Who the hell does she think she is? Suitable. I'll show her suitable."

"It's okay, honey. You're perfect for me," he said, suppressing a smile and planting a kiss on my check.

"But you have to think so. I'm your wife. Damn it! We're going on a diet. She thinks my weight is satisfactory now—just wait and see."

"What do you mean diet? I'm not going to have to eat cardboard again, am I?" Chuck asked with a pleading look.

Just then, Tania, my transplant coordinator, walked into the room and with a quizzical look, asked, "Is everything okay?"

"Yes, as long as you don't mind eating cardboard," Chuck moaned and sat back with his arms crossed over his belly defiantly.

"What do you mean?" asked Tania.

"Oh, nothing, he's just worried I'm going to take away his Oreos. We're fine. I just got a little worked up."

"Okay," she said, as Chuck glared at me.

"Dr. Peterson is running a little late so I'm going to take you to see the financial advisor, and then when you're finished with him, Dr. Peterson should be ready."

"Perfect!" I replied.

Chuck and I stood up to follow her when he whispered in my ear, "Why is it when you feel fat, I get punished? I have a perfect physique," he said, pointing to his round mid-section.

"Oh, you can keep your Oreos. Now, come on."

CHAPTER NINETEEN

"Start by doing what's necessary; then do what's possible; and suddenly you are doing the impossible." — Francis of Assisi

AFTER WE MET WITH THE financial advisor, Tania escorted us back to our room. "Dr. Peterson is finishing up with another patient, and he'll be in with you soon."

"Thank you, Tania." I replied as she closed the door behind her.

I was surprised when I looked over at Chuck, and he didn't have his phone in his hand. "What?" I asked.

"Do you think we'll be able to afford your being out of work for 6 to 8 weeks?"

"I'm sure we can swing it. I'll check with Loretta at work tomorrow to find out about short-term disability. I know it's part of my benefits, but I'll have to find out how much they pay. I'm sure God has a plan for our finances. He wouldn't ask me to do this if He didn't."

"At least, David's insurance pays for everything. I can't begin to imagine how much all this will cost," Chuck commented.

"I know. When Jackie explained about all the financial issues, I couldn't help but think of David. I read on one of the Facebook posts he's been out of work for a long time because of his illness. Chuck, wouldn't it be wonderful if I get approved for the transplant? I would be helping to change his life. It's amazing, isn't it?"

Flooded with emotions and images of David one day going back to work, tears slid down my cheek. And Chuck gently wiped them away with his finger.

"Yes, it'll be amazing. And you're amazing for wanting to do this. I'm a lucky man."

"As a matter-of-fact, yes, you are because I am pretty awesome—aren't I?"

"And humble too!" he smirked giving me an easy punch on the arm.

We were both laughing when Dr. Peterson walked into the room. "Hello, I'm Dr. Peterson."

"Hi, Dr. Peterson. I'm Amy, and this is my husband, Chuck."

"It's nice to meet you both. It looks like you've had a long day today—meeting with the whole transplant team, I see."

"Yes, I think we've met just about everyone but the janitor."

He chuckled and continued, "So, tell me a little about why you've decided to donate a kidney to, umm, David Ensley?" he asked as he flipped through a chart on his lap for the name.

Chuck's hand found mine as I told Dr. Peterson about the Facebook page David's sister had created and how I felt led to complete an application. I explained how Chuck knew the Ensley family from high school, but I hadn't met them, yet.

"Wow, what an incredible story. It does happen from time to time when strangers just want to help. I hope we can approve you because it's a good thing what you're doing. Have you been told anything about how this process works?"

"Tania has been fairly detailed I think..."

"But I have several questions for you," Chuck interrupted.

"Okay, ask me anything," the doctor replied.

"Will there be any long-term complications from the surgery for Amy? I understand you've been doing transplants for a while but what if something happens to her remaining kidney?"

"Both very good questions, Chuck."

Dr. Peterson repeated what Tania had told us earlier about when kidney transplants were first performed it was difficult for the donor. The surgeons would cut the donor from stem-to-sternum making the recovery time extremely long and challenging. But now, they operate microscopically, whenever possible, and the recovery time is approximately 6 to 8 weeks.

Dr. Peterson moved to a chart on the wall of a person's anatomy and showed us how the surgeon makes three incisions: two small incisions—one on the right side and another on the left side of the abdomen—and then a larger one from the belly button down to just above the pelvic bone. He inserts two rods containing surgical scissors and a camera into the smaller incisions and then cuts the arteries flowing to the kidney. Once the arteries are severed, the surgeon reaches his hand into the larger incision and extracts the kidney to give to the recipient's surgical team.

He explained that the donor and recipient lie in surgical suites side-by-side, and the kidney isn't removed until the recipient is 100 percent ready. Also, if anything were to happen to my remaining kidney, as a transplant donor, my name would go to the top of the national transplant list.

"Now I can't guarantee nothing will go wrong during surgery or in the future because there are always risks when a patient goes under anesthesia. But we've been doing this procedure at Carolinas Medical Center for over forty-years, and so far, we have not lost one donor."

"Well, good thing!" I said jokingly, and Chuck glared. I knew it wasn't funny for him.

Dr. Peterson continued, "Amy, I want you to understand this surgery is elective and as I said, there are risks. You may want to make sure you have all your affairs in order—like a will or advance directive, if any."

I nodded and said, "Yes, I understand. Jackie, the financial advisor, informed us and also, I shouldn't allow my health insurance to lapse because this surgery could be considered a pre-existing condition. But before we get into it, let's see if you approve me, first."

"Well, let's get on the examining table so I can take a look at you. Chuck, did I answer all your questions?"

"Yes, but I'm sure I'll have more."

"Ask me anything. Just stop me and we can discuss whatever you want," he replied, placing a cold stethoscope inside my shirt on my chest to listen to my heartbeat and then he moved it to my back.

"Take a few deep breaths for me."

I did as instructed and breathed in deeply a few times.

"Sounds good. Lie back for me, please."

He pushed on my stomach and sides for a few moments and then said, "The good news is it feels like you have two kidneys."

"Good thing, since I'll need one after I give one to David," I replied.

Then, he asked me to sit up and hang my feet over the sides, so he could check my reflexes. With a hard rubber object, he gave a quick hit to both my knees and my legs responded by kicking forward.

"Good reflexes. I like it, "he said nodding.

"Well, it looks like you're healthy. However, your blood pressure from earlier today was slightly elevated. I don't think it's anything to be concerned about because most people when they come into see me are a little anxious, which can cause the blood pressure to spike. But I would like to schedule you for a 24-hour blood pressure test just to rule out any potential issues."

"Okay, but normally, I have perfect blood pressure—nurses comment about it all the time. Should I be worried?" I asked.

"No, don't worry. As I said, you were probably nervous and it's to be expected. You'll wear a blood pressure cuff for 24 hours, and it'll take your vitals every 15 minutes. It's more bothersome than anything else because you'll need to wear it while sleeping. Would you mind if I send you to get one administered before you leave? I know it's one more stop but I'd like to get it done as soon as possible."

"Not a problem. We have time," I replied, scanning Chuck's face for any objections.

"Oh, and I almost forgot. We also need to perform a 24-hour urinalysis to determine your kidney function. Since it's Friday, it would be the ideal time to do both of the tests. We can start you on the blood pressure test today, and then you can begin the urinalysis Saturday morning. Can you bring both the blood pressure cuff and the urine samples back on Monday morning to the office? Tania will explain everything to you in more detail."

"Yes, I guess it'll be fine," I answered trying to imagine how

I'd bring 24 hours of urine samples back in on Monday. I giggled at the thought.

CHAPTER TWENTY

"Believe you can and you're halfway there."
—Theodore Roosevelt

CHUCK AND I HEADED TOWARD our car with two empty gallon-size plastic jugs and a plastic bowl-looking thing. Tania had given me detailed instruction about the 24-hour urinalysis. When I woke up Saturday morning, I needed to empty my bladder completely; then, afterward, begin to collect urine samples all day until the following morning.

As the sun shone brightly in the afternoon sky, I reached into my purse for my sunglasses. I drew in a slow, deliberate breath, and I thought, I can do this. It's only one day out of my life. Right?

A whistling sound caught my attention, and I glanced over at Chuck, who had the plastic bowl looking thing on his head.

"You're crazy! Why is it on your head?" I said, laughing hysterically.

"It looks like a hat." He paused to cast a devilish look over his shoulder.

"Yeah, okay. But you do realize I'm supposed to pee in the hat of yours come tomorrow morning?"

Fumbling the collection bowl off his head, he replied, "I know. I just wanted to make you laugh. It's been a long day."

"Yeah," I sighed. "How do you feel about things after meeting the doctor and all the other people?"

"Well, I'm still not thrilled about you having surgery, but I understand why you want to do it and as I continue to tell you, I'll support you either way."

The horn beeped, and the tail lights blinked on and off as Chuck unlocked the car. He lifted the trunk as we unloaded all my supplies for the weekend, before heading over to get prepped for the 24-hour blood pressure test.

"Chuck, I'm thankful to have you with me through this. I don't think I could—no, I wouldn't consider doing it without you."

"I know." Chuck met my eyes and slid his arms around my waist pulling me closer to him. "And you won't have to, either. For better or worse, right? You're my girl—I love you."

His lips softly grazed mine, and my heart fluttered upward at the tenderness of his words. How did I get so lucky to marry this man? Once a girlhood crush over which I doodled his name on my notebooks, he's now someone I couldn't live without.

After meeting with the social worker and then with the nephrologist, Chuck seemed more relaxed and open to the idea of me donating a kidney to David. I needed his support to do this.

"I love you, too."

Chuck swatted my butt and said, "Come on. We still have one more stop before we can go home. Do you have the directions Tania gave us?" He closed the trunk of the car and turned to follow me.

"Yup, it looks like it's near where we went for the X-rays this morning."

"Okay, lead the way."

Chuck and I walked in silence as we headed toward the main hospital building. He was right, today had been a long day.

I'm continually amazed how God knows what I need before I do. Part of me still thinks I'm certifiably nuts, and I'm probably very close. But then, the other part of me just knows I'm supposed to be David's donor. It was like knowing my name—I can't explain it.

I felt as if my purpose in life was to heal another human being. It was as if a part of me would be healed, too. The certainty I experienced could only come from God. He placed the desire to do this in my heart. I was so grateful He chose me for this incredible adventure. My heart raced at the thought, and it made me wonder what He had planned for me next.

CHAPTER TWENTY-ONE

"To a mind that is still, the whole universe surrenders." —Lao Tzu

HAVE YOU EVER HEARD THE saying, "Be careful what you wish for?" Well, it's true. I wondered what God had planned for me next and I shouldn't have asked. This blood pressure cuff on my arm wasn't the worst thing which had ever happened to me, but it wasn't pleasant either.

Every 15 minutes for a 24-hour period, the device would click, and then the cuff would squeeze my arm with what felt like a python squeezing all the oxygen out of my arm. Then, it would slowly tick down until I heard a long swooshing, and then it released the pressure in my arm.

I dreaded going to sleep. I'd only had it on for a few hours, and already I wanted to peel it off my arm. I was sure I'd be up all night which didn't make me happy. I kept trying to remind myself I this was all for a good cause, but honestly, I was having a hard time remembering why I wanted to subject myself to all this.

Maybe it wasn't such a good idea to agree to all this testing right now. On Sunday, both our families were coming over to celebrate Easter. I had a house to clean and dinner to prepare all while wearing this stupid blood pressure cuff and peeing in a jug all day while entertaining. What was I thinking?

I sat on the edge of the bed with my face cradled in my hands as tears trailed down my cheeks. I cried out to God, *"Why me? What makes You think I can do this? You picked the wrong person. I can't even endure a blood pressure cuff. What makes You think I'll survive surgery or living without two kidneys?"* Dread flowed cold inside me, and self-pity filled my soul.

Then a voice resounded in my ears, steady and clear, *"Amy, I got you. Lean on me. It'll be okay."* A sense of peace filled the room, and I knew everything would work out.

"Okay," I murmured.

Instantly, my fears vanished. Wiping my tear-stained cheeks with the back of my sleeve, I ran my fingers through my hair and headed downstairs for dinner.

We still hadn't told Alex or Chase about the possible kidney donation. I didn't want to worry them, especially Alex, until I knew for sure I was approved. Alex was my first-born and for many years it was just him and me. We had a special bond, and I knew he would understand my desire to donate, but I also knew he would worry needlessly.

Obviously, I had to tell them something about this intrusive thing on my arm. So, I told them the doctors wanted to monitor my blood pressure, but it was nothing to be concerned over. This seemed to satisfy both of them for the time being.

The 24-hour urinalysis was a different story. I knew I wouldn't be able to explain it away, so Chuck purchased a large cooler and plenty of ice to could keep the jug in the master bathroom instead of in the refrigerator. It was perfect, because the boys, for the most part, didn't go in our bathroom and it would allow me some much—needed privacy.

I suppressed a smile at the image of the boys finding a large jug of my pee in the refrigerator. It would be comical to see their reaction but, in the end, I decided it wouldn't be a good idea. It was better not to tell them or my family until we had real news to share.

As it turned out, my angels were working overtime to keep me comfortable because when I woke up Saturday morning, I felt more rested than I had in a long time.

As the fog began to lift, I remembered the pressure cuff on my arm, and immediately panic pooled inside me. I hope that stupid thing didn't fall off during the night. But then I heard the usual click and felt the tight pressure around my arm. A sense of relief came over me as I heaved a long sigh and lay my head back on my pillow. If it had fallen off during the night and I had to do it all over again, I would scream.

When I decided to submit an application to be a donor, I had no idea the amount of testing I would endure. One thing was for sure: if I had some mysterious illness, it would be found. In the end, I believed all this would be worth it.

Pulling myself out of bed, I made my way to the bathroom. As Tania instructed, I peed normally, but staring at the white plastic bowl, I knew my day would consist of countless trips to the bathroom.

CHAPTER TWENTY-TWO

"Faith can move mountains."—Matthew 17:20

THE WEEKEND FLEW BY, AND I managed to keep all the testing hidden in my master bathroom. As it turned out, the blood pressure monitoring wasn't as bad as I had anticipated. By Saturday afternoon, it was a distant memory. Even peeing in the jug wasn't as intrusive as I had envisioned.

On Sunday, we celebrated Easter with my family and enjoyed hamburgers and hot dogs while recounting old family stories on the patio—mostly of me and my wild teenage years. But then, I'd remind my mother that the police would show up at the house, not for me, but for my brother over stupid things like driving over a fire hydrant and leaving his car behind. Everyone was in high spirits with wine and food flowing freely.

Watching my family engaged in playful chatter, an uneasiness settled in me. What if they don't understand my calling to donate my kidney? What if they ask me not to do it? Would I be strong enough to continue without their support?

I reached for my wine, swirled it in the glass, and watched it go still as I contemplated telling them my secret. Chuck and I had decided to wait and see if I got approved first because otherwise they would worry needlessly. But a sliver of guilt needled me as I participated in a loving pastime with my family. I was lying to them, but did they have the right to know?

Lost in my thoughts, I barely recognized my mother's voice as she called my name. "Amy, are you alright? You seem a million miles away."

"Oh, yes, Mom. I'm fine. Just have a lot on my mind."

"Well, when you're ready to have us leave, just say the word."

"No, Mom. Please stay. I'm enjoying everyone being here."

Alex piped up, "Mom's probably worried about the blood pressure test thing she had to take this weekend. Although she said it's nothing."

I shot a pleading look toward Chuck, who looked startled by Alex's words, too.

Chuck immediately answered, "You're right, Alex. But your Mom's okay. It's just routine testing. Her blood pressure was a little high at the appointment the other day, and the doctors thought it could be 'white-coat syndrome.' Nothing to worry about—right, Linda?" He directed the question to my mother.

"Yes, it's a common thing to happen at a doctor's office, and they usually order it to eliminate false testing. Has your blood pressure ever been high before, Amy?"

I hadn't realized I had been holding my breath until I tried to answer her. Attempting to calm my racing heart I replied, "No, it was a little high at this last visit, and the doctor wanted more testing. I thought it was a little excessive, but I'm sure the test will come back fine." I shrugged my shoulders insinuating it wasn't a big deal.

I felt the blood rise in my cheeks and was grateful when Chase, with smooth teenage swagger, asked his Aunt Fran if he could have a piece of the red velvet cake she brought. We all laughed because he could sweet talk anyone as if it was second nature and, of course, Aunt Fran couldn't resist a request from either of her "boys" as she affectionately called them.

"Sure," she said with a wink and got up as Chase followed her inside.

Feeling saved for the moment, I asked, "Would anyone like some coffee with dessert?"

A few hours later as everyone left, we closed the door on the last guest. I fell into Chuck's arms. "I'm so glad that's over," I said.

"I know. Me, too."

"Thank you for the save this afternoon. Good thinking, turning the question on my mom. You know you're sexy when you're lying your butt off," I teased, giving him a kiss.

"You're welcome. Leave it to Alex to bring up the blood pressure testing."

"I know, but he didn't know to keep quiet. I'm just glad my mother didn't ask any questions. I wasn't ready to tell them about the donation yet, although I contemplated it for a few minutes." Chuck gave me a quizzical look.

"I know we decided to wait to see if I get approved, but I felt guilty lying to my family. Do you think they'll understand?"

Chuck led me over to the couch, and as I cuddled in beside him, he replied, "When the time is right, we'll tell them, and I'm sure they'll understand—they love you."

"I know. I just worry."

"It'll all work out. Close your eyes and relax." He stroked my hair softly as my eyes started to flutter shut, and then exhaustion overtook me as I slipped off to sleep.

PART THREE

CHAPTER TWENTY-THREE

"Sometimes the smallest things take up the most room in your heart." —Winnie the Pooh

A BRIGHT WHITE LIGHT BLINDED me as I blinked the room into focus. At first, I thought I was in heaven. Then someone bent over me with a sweet, blurry face. "You're awake. Good. The surgery is over, and I'm getting ready to take you to your room now."

Thousands of questions spiraled through my mind, but I felt powerless to form any of them into words. So, I briefly nodded my head and closed my eyes.

When I woke the second time, a nurse had rolled me into

my room and was locking the wheels of my bed. I wanted to ask where Chuck was, when the door opened pouring light in from the corridor and there he was. He stood motionless and, as his gaze met mine, it was as if we were the only two people in the world. From his expression, I knew the surgery was a success. Perks of giggles flowed from me as he rushed over to kiss me with an urgency causing me to bite my lower lip.

"Hey, easy, easy," I mumbled.

"I'm sorry. I was afraid I'd never see you again. I love you," and he kissed me again only this time more softly.

"I love you, too. How's David?" My head felt fuzzy, and my mouth felt as if I had cotton balls wedged in my cheeks.

"He's good. He's in ICU for the night and should be in his room tomorrow morning. We can see him then. Amy, your kidney peed all over the doctor," Chuck proudly exclaimed. "I have pictures."

"You have what?" I said amused. Chuck was ecstatic, and I could tell by his enthusiasm he was relieved and proud all at the same time.

"Yes, the doctor gave us pictures. I'll get them."

The nurse who brought me from recovery finished attaching all the equipment and said, "Your nurse will be in with you momentarily."

I nodded and as she left the room, my mother walked in.

"Not to interrupt, but can Mom and Pops come in?"

"Of course! Yes, come in," I replied groggily.

A slice of colored sunlight fell on my mother as she leaned over the bed railing and gently kissed my cheek. "I'm so proud of you, Amy. They said David is doing well and his body has accepted your kidney. They'll need to watch him for signs of rejection, but we're told they aren't expecting it to happen."

A sense of relief filled me. David's body rejecting the new kidney was something I worried about, and David and Susanne too, but so far God had showered us with His amazing blessing. We were both going to be okay.

"And how are you feeling?" Mom asked.

"I'm not sure. I can't really feel anything yet, which may be a gift. I'm sleepy and I don't feel like I could lift my head off the pillow. How long did it take?"

"About two and a half hours from the time they took you back until you went into recovery. The doctors came in to tell us after your part of the surgery was over. And we had live updates on the computer screen informing us of your status at all times," Mom replied.

"Yeah, it was kind of like the Domino's tracker telling us when our pizza would be ready," Pops said with a smirk. I loved Pops. He always has a quirky way about making me feel better. He married my mother after I moved out of the house, which is why I think we got along so well—he didn't have to live with me as a teenager.

"Thanks, Pops. I'm glad I remind you of a pizza!"

Chuck came back over to show me the pictures of my kidney peeing. To be honest, I didn't want to see them. When the surgeon explained the procedure to us, Chuck was more interested than me. My only concern had been to make sure the doctor knew not to drop anything important on the floor and not to leave anything behind which didn't belong to me. Otherwise, I didn't care to know which organs, if any, would need to be moved to reach the kidney, nor did I want to look at pictures of my kidney peeing on the doctor. But Chuck loved information such as this, which is why we made such a great team.

Suddenly, a woman in green scrubs scurried into the room. Removing a stethoscope from around her neck, she said, "Hi, my name is Kim and I'm your nurse. I need to take your vitals and give you some medicine. How are you feeling, Amy?"

"I'm good so far, I think. I'm tired, but otherwise I'm in no pain at the moment. Could I have some water?"

"How about some ice chips? I'll get it for you in a moment and set up a PCA pump as soon as I can. Did the doctors tell you what it is?"

I nodded and said, "Yes, they told me about it, but I don't remember much right now."

Suppressing a smile, Kim responded, "Not a problem. I'll explain it when I get it hooked up in a few minutes." She continued to take my blood pressure and pulse. Then she stuck a thermometer in my mouth and after a long beep withdrew it and disposed of the plastic covering it. "I'll be right back."

"Where's Granna and PopPop?' I asked.

"They are on the way up. They needed to make a stop on the way. Fran is with them," said Mom.

"Has anyone called the boys to tell them I'm doing okay?"

"I did, and I told them to wait until tomorrow to come see you. I didn't want them driving into uptown and then trying to drive home in the dark. It's too easy to get lost in the wrong section of town at night," Chuck said.

"I agree. I just wanted to make sure they knew I was awake from surgery and fine." My eyes closed involuntarily but I could still hear everyone talking. My mind seemed fuzzy and disjointed. I wanted to talk but no matter how much I willed myself to open my eyes, my body wasn't responding. So, I finally gave into the darkness and drifted off.

CHAPTER TWENTY-FOUR

"Nothing is impossible, the word itself says 'I'm possible'!" — Audrey Hepburn

I BLINKED AS FRAGMENTS OF images slowly started coming into focus. It took a moment to remember where I was, but then I felt the warmth of Chuck's hand covering mine. I smiled, realizing he'd sat beside me in a loving vigil while I slept.

"Hey, there. You've been asleep for a while. How are you feeling?" he asked brushing a piece of hair out of my face.

"I'm not sure yet. What time is it?"

"It's about six."

"Where is everyone?"

"They left a couple of hours ago. They wanted to get some dinner but said they'd be back in the morning. I think your mom was tired, and I know my parents were, too."

"How's David?" I asked, sitting up gingerly. Chuck reached to adjust the pillow behind my head, trying to make me more comfortable.

"He's doing fine. So far, no rejection. They have him in ICU at least until tomorrow morning. Jennifer came by to see you while you were sleeping."

"This has been a long journey for her, too. Did she say she'd be back tonight? I'd like to see her."

"No, probably not until tomorrow."

"Okay. Hey, what about you? Have you gotten any rest?" I asked, caressing his hand.

"No, not yet. I wanted to make sure my girl was all right, first. I wanted to see those beautiful blue eyes. I felt a little nervous because you slept so long, but the nurse told me it was normal. So, I've been sitting here waiting for you to wake up."

I wanted to cry at his words. I married an amazing man who loved me. What more could I ask for than the love of this guy? I waited a long time for him to come back into my life and had experienced many failed relationships along the way. But I'm grateful for the heartache because I appreciate Chuck even more now.

Many times, I've wondered what would have happened if we had married as teenagers. Would we still be married, or would we have been divorced before we were twenty?

I remembered the time in high school I asked him to take me to see Dirty Dancing with Patrick Swayze. He adamantly refused.

"It's a chick movie, and I won't be caught dead watching it," he replied. His words broke my heart, and I couldn't understand his cruel reaction.

But now, before me sat a man who cherished me and would do anything for me—including watching *Dirty Dancing*.

"Hey, do you remember our first date when we got back together after twenty years?" I asked him.

"How could I forget? You roped me into watching a terrible Patrick Swayze movie—*Dirty Dancing*, and then fell asleep on me five minutes into it. I couldn't even reach my beer on the coffee table because I was afraid I'd wake you up."

"Ouch! Don't make me laugh. It hurts," I winced and lightly applied pressure on the bandages covering my stomach, trying to keep the pain from exploding.

"Yeah, well, you deserve it. You didn't wake up until the credits started rolling, and my arm was so numb it took hours afterward for it to feel normal again."

"You should've taken me to see it when I asked you the first time in high school."

"Oh, no way it would've happened. Could you imagine my reputation if I was seen there?"

"What reputation?"

"What do you mean—my cool status, of course," Chuck said, puffing out his chest like a rooster.

"Oh yeah, you were so cool. But I think the word 'cool' is out of date now, honey."

"What are you talking about, I was amazing."

"I know, it's why I fell asleep on you," I teased.

"Oh, you know how to cut right through the heart," he replied, grabbing his chest and pretending to fall over the side of the chair.

"You'll survive."

We were both laughing as Kim, my nurse, came in and asked, "What's so funny?"

"Amy thinks it's funny to destroy my ego."

"Well, this must've been an interesting conversation, but I'm not going to touch it." She smiled at Chuck and then said to me, "I'm glad to see you're awake, Amy. How are you feeling? On a scale of zero to ten, with ten being extremely painful and zero no pain at all, what is your pain level?"

"I'd say about a five. I feel pressure around my stomach, but it's better now."

"Good, it means your pain is manageable at the moment. While you were sleeping, I hooked up the PCA pump I told you about earlier through the IV. It's setup for you to administer morphine dosages every fifteen minutes. All you need to do is push this button," she said and handed me a long cord with a round, silver button on the top of it.

I looked at the button and my gaze followed the cord up to a square box attached to the IV in my arm.

"If you're not feeling any pain after fifteen minutes, try waiting a little while longer before giving yourself another dose. But don't try to be superwoman because if your pain gets out of control, it'll make it much harder to get it under control. Although, the less you need to use the pump, the faster you can go home. It's a fine line, but do you understand?"

"Yes, I understand and trust me I'm not superwoman—I don't like pain. Would it be okay if I pushed the button now?"

"Of course, we gave you a shot of morphine while you were sleeping but it's about time for another dose."

I pushed the button, and immediately I felt warmth spreading from the IV up and down my arm and then, the next thing I knew, I was completely relaxed—absolutely no pain. I looked over at Chuck and smiled.

"Hey, honey!" I said reaching for his hand.

"Keep in mind, Amy, you can only push the button every fifteen minutes but no more than five times every two-hours. The pump is programmed to give you a set dosage, and it won't go over the limit. Let me know if your pain increases or if you need anything else."

"I think we're good for now," Chuck responded.

"Okay, I'll check back in a little while."

But before leaving, she placed a clear plastic handheld device in front of me and said, "I almost forgot—to keep you from developing pneumonia, you need to breathe using this Incentive Spirometer, which is a fancy name for a breathing device. See this black line here?" she asked, pointing to a line made with a fat magic marker.

I nodded.

"You need to make the yellow ball rise to meet this line by inhaling and then holding it for five seconds."

No problem—piece of cake, I thought.

"Go ahead and give it a try. First, exhale completely and then slowly and deeply inhale covering the mouthpiece."

I took a quick breath and released it completely. Then I placed my lips around the tube attached to the device and attempted to inhale. The incisions in my stomach felt as if they were ripping apart while the yellow ball remained motionless.

"Not as easy as you thought?" Kim responded.

"No, it hurt!" My voice was barely audible as pain seared through the lower region of my abdomen.

"It'll hurt but push through it. It'll help you expand your lungs and cough up any secretions keeping the lungs clear. You're to practice this at least ten times every hour when awake. Got it?"

My eyes widened at her instructions. Ten times! There's no

way. I gave it all I had, and the blasted yellow ball didn't move. Thank God for the pain pump. I so wanted to push the button again, but I knew it was too soon. Damn!

"Yes, I understand. Of course, I'll do it, but nobody told me about this fun part."

"It's critical because it'll help you get home faster. Also, you're on a clear liquid diet tonight. You should receive something to eat soon. If you need anything, push the red button on the remote and someone at the nurses' station will find me. Or you can call my cell number posted on the whiteboard by the door."

Kim handed me a large, clunky remote which was attached to my bed by a long expanding cord. At first glance, I noticed it not only controlled the TV channels and volume but also had call buttons for the nurses' station and one labeled 911 in case of an emergency.

"Thank you, Kim. We appreciate your help," Chuck said, and I smiled in agreement.

Kim nodded and then with a quiet click the door closed behind her.

CHAPTER TWENTY-FIVE

"No act of kindness, no matter how small, is ever wasted." —Aesop

"IT'LL BE ALRIGHT, AMY. YOU'LL get the ball to the line in no time," Chuck said. I wasn't sure if he was trying to reassure himself or me.

"Yeah, I hope so." I looked at the stupid ball, and my shoulders sagged in temporary defeat. Years before, I had been an avid runner which requires deep lung capacity. Why then was it so hard for me to inhale and get the blasted ball to move?

The pain in my abdomen was intense, and I desperately wanted to push the button on the pain pump again. But as Kim had so kindly reminded me, I had to wait fifteen minutes between each injection, and after studying the long arm on the wall clock, I had eight more minutes to go.

"Although there's nothing which would've changed my mind

about donating my kidney to David, I wish I would've known about this breathing torture apparatus beforehand, so I could've prepared for it. You know? There was a lot of information I would've liked to have known before."

"I thought you researched everything?"

"Of course, I did, but little things like this I wouldn't have found in a kidney donation brochure."

There was a gentle knock at the door. "Anyone ready for dinner in here?"

"Yes, please come in," I replied, attempting to wiggle myself up into a more comfortable sitting position.

A lovely, plump woman with a beaming smile came through the door holding a tray. She had long black hair swept back in a loose ponytail and smoky green eyes which lit up her face. She placed the tray on the table in front of me and raised it so it would roll over my lap.

Lifting the top of one of the bowls, she said, "Well, it looks like you have delicious beef broth as your entrée tonight and, oh look here, yummy green Jell-O for desert."

"Oh, boy! I can't wait." I picked up the spoon and gently ran it through the brown, dull liquid. I thought to myself was this made from an actual beef bone or one of those little cubes my mom would use to make broth when I was sick. Either way, it didn't matter, I wasn't very hungry, and this brown liquid didn't make my mouth water.

"Don't worry, tomorrow you'll be on a regular diet. Would you like eggs in the morning or French toast?"

I gave her a puzzled look, and she replied, "We try to get your order for the next day when we bring dinner. And I know asking you about regular food is probably not the nicest thing I could do, but just think, in a few short hours you can have watery eggs or hard French Toast."

I didn't answer her for several beats because I was trying not to laugh—my incisions still raw with pain.

"Oh, I'm sorry. I guess I shouldn't make jokes. I'm sure it hurts to laugh, but as they say humor is the best medicine, right?"

"Yes, you're right. I will have some watery eggs with a side of hard toast, so I can throw it at my husband."

"Hey, now wait a minute, how did I get pulled into this," Chuck responded, looking up from his phone.

"It's okay, Honey. I'm not going to throw food at you. I was just checking to see if you're still alive over there."

"Yeah, well, whatever," Chuck said and turned his attention back to the game on his phone.

"Don't mind him," I replied to the aide.

"No problem. What would you like for lunch? There's grilled chicken or chicken salad and for dinner meatloaf with mashed potatoes or salmon with grilled asparagus."

"Hmm. Let me think; everything sounds good. Chicken

salad for lunch and salmon with asparagus for dinner and then, of course, eggs for breakfast."

"Perfect. I got you down. Enjoy the broth tonight, and someone will be by in the morning with your breakfast."

"Thank you for your help."

"You're welcome."

I stared at the lukewarm beef broth and green Jell-O and leaned in to taste the broth. As the bitter beef flavor lingered in the back of my throat, I wondered if my taste buds would ever be normal again. Even though I wasn't hungry and the broth less than appetizing, I knew I should probably eat something with all these narcotics. I glanced at the clock. Three more minutes before my next round. Would three minutes make such a big difference, I wondered. I mean, would the pain medicine kill me with only minutes to go? What could be the harm?

I reached for the round button and stared at it for a minute. Surely a few minutes early wouldn't matter. I glanced over at Chuck and saw his attention given entirely to the game on his phone, so I pushed the button with the intent of feeling the same rush of endorphins I did the last time. But I felt nothing—absolutely nothing. Damn!

CHAPTER TWENTY-SIX

"Be still and know that I Am God." —Psalm 40:10

AS THE MOONLIGHT STREAMED THROUGH the window, I rubbed my eyes trying to blink the room back into focus. I must have fallen asleep after my last dose of pain medicine. I smiled as I remembered the disappointment when the button didn't work with only a few minutes to go. I guess they don't want me to overdose and I should feel grateful, but seriously it was only three minutes, I thought.

I looked at the clock and decided I could give myself another dosage, so I patted around the bed, feeling for the magic button. Panic filled me, and my eyes grew large.

"Are you looking for this?" Chuck asked, holding the pump in his hands.

"Yes. Thank you." I reached for it, and Chuck playfully pulled it back with a twinkle in his eye. I scowled.

"Here you go. I was just joking. Don't take my head off. If looks could kill, I'd be six feet under right now."

"It wasn't funny," I replied.

"Yes, it was." Chuck sat down in the chair beside my bed.

I hit the button, and the familiar feeling washed over me. I felt my body sink into the bed as my mind fell into a trance-like state. I laid my head back on my pillow for a moment and closed my eyes. No pain. I knew I needed to start extending the periods between dosages, but the pain had been more than I expected. To be honest, I didn't give the pain much thought when I decided to do this, but now I wished I had.

I wouldn't have changed my mind in any case. David had a future now; whereas, twenty-four hours ago, his life, was coming to a tragic end. His family had told me they didn't think he would live much longer without a transplant.

As I lay there, my eyes fluttered shut for a moment when suddenly I sat up straight and asked, "What's today's date?"

"July 6th, why?"

"It's early." I felt a distinct dampness. My body had turned against me, I thought. Why? This was something I hadn't considered a possibility when I pictured this day in my head. I could usually tell by the minute when my monthly friend would visit, and this was unlike her to arrive five days early.

"What's early?"

"My period!" I laid my head back on my pillow and threw my

hands over my head, this was the last thing I needed, or thought would have happened. It was five days early. Why? Why God? Couldn't You had let this wait until I got home?

"Would you get a nurse for me, Chuck? I need something for it. I didn't bring anything with me because I wasn't expecting it for another week."

Chuck reached for the TV remote, which had the nurses' station call button on it and pushed the button. We heard three short rings and then a sweet southern voice said, "Hello, this is the nurses' station. How can I help you?"

"Can you send Kim into our room, please?" Chuck asked.

"Yes, is everything alright?"

"Yes, we just need her assistance."

"Okay. She'll be in shortly."

"Thank you, Chuck," I whispered.

"It'll be okay. Kim will help you get it taken care of."

"No, I want you to help me, please?"

Chuck's face stiffened, and his eyes widened in a sudden panic as he absently twirled his wedding band. "What do you mean? Wha...what do I need to do?"

"I'm not sure yet. I don't think the panties I brought with me will fit over my belly. Hopefully, they have something." I placed my hands on my belly amazed at how full it felt. I assumed it was from all the air the doctor told me they would use so they could see everything clearly.

Kim appeared in the doorway. "What's going on? Everything okay?"

"I got my period. It wasn't due for another week, so I didn't think to even bring anything with me."

"It's okay, this happens sometimes. Your body just went through a major ordeal, and now it's relaxed. It happens. We'll get you taken care of."

"I still have a catheter. Do you think we could take it out? Also, I don't know if the panties I brought will fit me because my stomach is extended and bloated."

"We can probably take the catheter out tomorrow morning after the doctor comes by to see you. But for now, I'll give you a pad and a pair of hospital panties. It's common for your stomach to be enlarged some because of the air they use to blow everything up."

Humiliated, I looked over at Chuck. "Is this a cruel joke? Why couldn't this have waited? It wasn't how I thought this would play out. Couldn't I get a pass for a few days?"

Chuck tried to reassure me it would work out. Life wasn't over, and he'd do what he could to help me.

Kim returned to the room with all the items I requested and a change of sheets.

"Let's get you up and into the bathroom."

Kim lowered the bed as far as it would go and then placed her arm under my left arm. She gently guided me as I stood up for the first time since the surgery early in the morning. I waited for a minute to allow the feeling in my head to even out. Then, she helped me walk the three steps to the bathroom, which felt like ten miles.

"Okay. While you're in there, I'll change your sheets." She also placed a new gown on the table in the bathroom. "You'll need this, too."

"Thank you," I mumbled in embarrassment. My head held down, I entered the bathroom with a tall pole on wheels which held the pain pump, the IV, and the catheter bag. The door closed gently behind me.

CHAPTER TWENTY-SEVEN

"What we think we become." — **Buddha**

MY EYES OPENED SLOWLY, AND I heard the familiar, yet soothing sound of gargled breathing. I turned my head slightly left and saw Chuck lying cramped in chair which folded out into tiny bed. The room came with an adjoining alcove which included a TV and a couch where he could sleep more comfortably but he insisted on staying close to me. While I found his gesture endearing, the awkward way his neck hung over the side of the chair I knew he wasn't having a restful sleep.

My room was larger than I had expected—a suite, in fact. I was told donors received the "Presidential" suite. The bathroom was just to the right of my bed with a long vanity and sink beside it. A wide-screen TV hung from the entrance way to alcove. Chairs were scattered about from all the visitors I had yesterday.

A heavy-set, middle-aged nurse came in and whispered, "It's

okay. I'm here to get your vitals. Unfortunately, we have to check on you, but I'll try not to wake you. Go back to sleep."

I nodded as exhaustion pulled me back to sleep. The first day after surgery was harder than I'd anticipated. Silently, I prayed the doctors would agree to remove the catheter in the morning.

When I finally awoke, Chuck was flipping through the channels on the TV.

"Good morning. Were you able to get any sleep?" I asked, my voice barely audible, dry from the night's sleep.

The morning sun beamed through the blinds. "I've slept better, but I'm okay. This bed-chair thing is not as comfortable as it looks."

"You should go home tonight and sleep in bed. You don't need to stay here with me all night long."

"No way. When a Cunningham is in the hospital, then another Cunningham is with them the entire time which, my dear, is me. I'm here for the duration. However, I may go home and shower when your parents get here if you don't mind."

I pinched the crook of my nose to keep the tears from coming. I loved my husband so much.

After I made it into the bathroom the night before, I couldn't get undressed because I couldn't bend over. Chuck quietly helped me clean up and even disposed of everything.

"Hey, now, there's no need for tears. I'll be back," he teased.

"No, I want you to go home and get some rest—take a shower. I just don't know how to thank you for last night."

"Of course. You are my girl and being by your side is where I belong." He kissed the tip of my nose and gently brushed back the wisps of hair which had fallen across my eyes. "I love you more than you know. You are an amazing woman."

A gentle rapping at the door brought us both back to the present as Dr. Peterson and an older man with a head full of shocking white hair which matched his doctor's coat walked into my room.

"How are you this morning, Amy? I'd like to introduce you to Dr. Wheatherby. He's working on my service today. I don't believe you've met him before."

"I think I'm good—just waking up. Can I get the catheter out today?"

"Possibly. I heard you had a little inconvenience last night but don't worry about it. Unfortunately, it happens more than you think. Let me examine you first, and then we'll talk about removing the catheter. Okay?"

"Okay," I murmured as my face lost three shades of color. My nurse had told him about my getting my period.

Dr. Peterson pulled the blankets off me and lifted my gown as he pushed the button on the side of my bed to raise it. He placed a cold stethoscope on my stomach and listened. "Have you experienced any gas yet?"

Oh my God, what did he just ask me? My head reeled with embarrassment. "Um, no not really—some I guess. I feel bloated, though."

"Well, it means things haven't started to wake up in your intestines and stomach. We should probably wait another day before removing the catheter. When we give you anesthesia for surgery, not only does it put you to sleep, but your organs also, as well as the bowels and bladder. It may take another day for everything to start working properly."

"Okay," I replied in a low, disappointed voice.

"I know it wasn't the answer you were hoping for, but trust me, waiting another day will be better than removing the catheter only to put it back in again. It puts you at a greater risk for infection. On a positive side, your incisions look great. They are healing well."

"Good news! Do you know when I can take my wife home?" asked Chuck.

"Not for a few more days yet. If we can take the catheter out tomorrow and she comes off the pain pump, I think it's possible she can go home by Saturday or Sunday at the latest."

Dr. Wheatherby peered at me through wire-rimmed glasses, "You're healing nicely. Don't try to push yourself too much but you do need to walk some today. We like for our patients to be walking the day after surgery. It helps to get everything moving as Dr. Peterson mentioned."

My eyes widened. How could I possibly walk with all this equipment attached to me and not to mention my butt hanging out of this nightgown for all the world to see? I don't remember packing a bathrobe, and, oh, my hair, I thought, as I tried to run my fingers through it... did I remember a brush?

I knew I was acting silly, but I couldn't stop these wacky thoughts and emotions from bubbling up like a volcano. Things were not going as planned but, to be honest, I couldn't remember what the plan was exactly.

Pulling my emotions back in check, I asked, "How far do I need to walk? I have all this equipment attached to me."

"We don't want you running a marathon, but you should walk as far as possible. At first, a lap around the nurses' station is fine, and then as you get stronger, you can increase it to two laps and then so on. Don't worry about the pain pump and IV; it'll go with you. You can lean on it to walk, or someone can move it while you use a walker. The point is to move. Okay?"

I was speechless for several moments, but Dr. Wheatherby's voice was so kind and encouraging, it caused hope to rise within me. I thought maybe I could do this. It was just a lap around the nurses' station, right?

"Okay, I'll do it."

A sweet smell of pancakes and eggs filled the room as the nurse's aide brought in my breakfast tray. "Well, then, I think it's our cue to leave. Amy, if you need us, just ask your nurse to page us, and we'll stop by but I'm sure you'll do fine. We'll be back tomorrow morning."

"Thank you, Dr. Peterson, Dr. . Will you always come by this early?" I glanced at the clock on the wall, and the long arm read seven o'clock.

"Yes, we get started early. I like to see my patients between 6 and 7 a.m. before surgeries begin. But I'm always available if you need me."

As the doctors left, the nurse's aide placed the tray on the table in front of me. She lifted the top off my entrée and said, "Enjoy." She was petite with red hair wild around her face and hazel oval eyes, beautiful at only eighteen or nineteen.

"Thank you," I replied. I decided not to tell her I didn't order pancakes, only eggs, because she looked so sweet and I didn't want to make any trouble for her. Besides, if they tasted as good as they smelled, I'd be happy.

She smiled at Chuck and then left.

"Honey, if you want to go home and rest for a little while, I'll be okay. You said Mom would be here early, and I'm sure your parents will be here anytime. Besides, after I eat, I'll probably try to sleep for a while."

"No, I'll wait for someone to get here. I don't want to leave you alone."

My stomach growled in anticipation of the food. I hadn't

eaten anything substantial for three days and I sure didn't count last night's beef broth and Jell-O a fulfilling meal.

I opened the syrup package and dipped a forkful of pancakes into it. Then as I lifted my fork dripping with pancakes and syrup to my mouth, I heard in her typical sweet, southern draw "How's my favorite daughter-in-law this morning?"

CHAPTER TWENTY-EIGHT

"You must do the things you think you cannot do."
—Eleanor Roosevelt

CHUCK LEFT TO REST AND shower shortly after his parents arrived. I asked him to grab my bathrobe while he was there and a few other essentials I forgot. I should have been more specific on the bathrobe I wanted because when he returned, he brought my ugly green, gray and yellow plaid robe I rescued from the Goodwill years ago.

The raggedy green robe had hung on the back of the bathroom door beside a soft purple robe—one more fitting for strangers to see. "You're always wearing it, so I thought it was your favorite," Chuck stated with obvious guy logic.

I wanted to yell but what good would it do? His face beamed with accomplishment.

Chuck lowered the bed as far as it would go and then helped

me maneuver my legs around, so I could stand up. Fear seized my stomach with a tight clench. I was attempting to walk to the nurses' station and back, but, I doubted my strength, or endurance, to make it there.

But my parents, Chuck's parents, and Fran, were there to help me and although I knew the nurses' station wasn't far, to me it felt like miles.

My defenses melted away as a picture filled my mind of us all parading down the hall together. My mother-in-law, in her late seventies walked, with a visible limp and relied on a walker to get around, and my father-in-law, although relatively healthy, had a slow gait. And then, there was me in the ugly green bathrobe pushing an IV tower and relying on my seventy-year-old father-in-law for support.

A sob caught in my throat as a moment of gratitude filled me. Where would I be without my family? I loved them all.

I placed my feet on the ground and stood for the second time since surgery the day before. The room spun at an accelerated speed but eventually my head caught up, and my balance equaled out. I felt queasy but ready to walk.

"Take your time, Amy. You'll feel dizzy at first," Mom said as she held my gown closed in the back and Chuck fitted the ugly green bathrobe around my arms. I felt grateful that at least my backside was not on display for the world to see.

Mom moved the IV tower closer to me, so I could steady

myself. PopPop, my father-in-law, offered me his arm, and then Mom asked, "Are you ready?"

"As ready as I'll ever be, I guess."

The first few steps came slowly. Each movement was a deliberate action on my part to will my feet and legs to move. Granna walked beside me on the right with her walker and PopPop on my left steadying my arm.

It felt like years had passed before we finally made it to the nurses' station. "You're halfway there," Mom chimed in, and I shot her a glaring look. Her positive motivation wasn't helping at the moment.

"Can we stop for a minute? I need to catch my breath. It's a lot harder than it looks and to think a few years ago I ran marathons. Now I'm praying I make it back to my room before collapsing."

"But you're doing good. You're almost done for this round," Mom chirped.

"Yeah and I get to do it again—can't wait!"

"Oh, come on. Let's get you back to bed," she responded.

"I wonder if David is in a room yet, or is he still in ICU?" I asked.

"I think he was supposed to be moved later this afternoon. If you're up to it, maybe we can visit this evening," Chuck said.

"I'd love it. Will you find out when David will be moved?"

"I will. Go with your mom and the gang. I'll meet you back in the room."

"Thank you, Honey. I love you." He gave me a quick peck on the lips and, grinning, headed off to find out information about David.

"Okay, guys. Let's get 'er done!" I cheered and at a turtle's pace we headed back to my room.

CHAPTER TWENTY-NINE

"Our deepest fear is not that we are inadequate. Our deepest fear is that we are powerful beyond measure. It is our light, not our darkness that most frightens us." — Marianne Williamson (A Return to Love: Reflections on the Principles of "A Course in Miracles")

AFTER SETTLING BACK INTO BED, it was time for another dose of pain medication. I reached for my favorite button on the long table beside me and pushed it, waiting in anticipation of the familiar feeling of ecstasy to wash over me. Although I used it for pain, I could easily see how people could become addicted. They would begin innocently with some pain they wanted to numb, but then the happy dream could turn into a nightmare.

Unfortunately, as I previously mentioned, addiction wasn't foreign to me. As a teenager, I became addicted to cocaine. Drugs temporarily masked the pain I carried deep within me. All my young life, I had searched for a place to belong; something which made me whole. The effects of being molested as a child, and my parents' subsequent divorce afterward, left me feeling incomplete and less than human.

I always related to the fairy-tale, Pinocchio. Like the wooden marionette, I craved someone or something to love me enough to make me a real person. In the story, however, the Blue Fairy told Pinocchio he could only become a real boy if he could prove himself to be "brave, truthful and unselfish." But along his path, he met people and situations who pulled him into unsavory situations and challenged his desire to be a "real boy."

Pinocchio found himself on vacation in Pleasure Island, where without rules or authority, Pinocchio and the other boys partied, drank, and gambled. Jiminy, Pinocchio's conscience, discovered Pleasure Island was cursed, and eventually all the boys on the island turned into donkeys and were sold into slavery. When Jiminy returned to Pleasure Island to tell Pinocchio, he found the other boys completely transformed into terrifying donkeys. With the help of Jiminy, Pinocchio escaped Pleasure Island, only partially changed.

Cocaine had been my Pleasure Island and my mother, my conscience. I found myself drinking, smoking, and doing drugs, completely unaware of the curse of addiction. I did things I wouldn't have normally done and eventually began to transform into a partial donkey and almost sold into slavery as a drug addict. Drugs were my first thought in the morning and my last thought as I passed out from the drugs at night. Every minute during the day was consumed with how and where to get more cocaine.

Like Pinocchio, I lied. My nose didn't grow, but it should have. I compulsively lied to use drugs and stay on Pleasure Island. One time, I told a lie so convincing my Grandmother thought I was a hero. The truth, however, was I couldn't see her during her visit because I was too busy cashing checks I stole from friends and strangers, so I could smoke cocaine.

Because of this behavior, I never expected God to use me for such a profound purpose. I came to believe in God shortly after my son was born, and through God's love my life changed. I still wondered, however: if people knew of all the bad things I had done, would they laugh at me for even considering becoming a living donor. But one of my favorite quotes is by St. Francis of Assisi—*"I have been all things unholy; if God can work through me, he can work through anyone."*

God told me He would use me to save David's life. Who was I to argue?

Raw emotion welled up in my throat as I watched this miracle unfold in my hospital room. My mother laughed at some story Granna was telling, as my husband absently twisted the cap on his Diet Coke bottle. PopPop sat close to Granna and Fran, grinning magnetically, and gently stroking my hand. Besides Chuck and my mom, Fran had been my biggest supporter for the donation. She understood my need to obey God's calling on my life and did whatever she could to help.

Filled with joy, I closed my eyes, *"Thank you, Papa. Once I was lost, but now I'm found. You took the lowly and the humble, and You did an amazing thing. You used me to save another's life but, in the process, You also saved mine. And now here we are. I'm without words!"*

CHAPTER THIRTY

"The best and most beautiful things in the world cannot be seen or even touched—they must be felt with the heart." —Helen Keller

I AWOKE THE NEXT MORNING to a hum of activity in my room. The clock on the wall read an ungodly six a.m. Pulling the covers over my face, I screamed in my head, "Nooooo!"

Samantha, my nurse's aide, whistled a song I knew but couldn't place while she attached a pressure cuff to my arm and took the usual vitals. "Good morning, Sunshine. Glad to see you awake."

I nodded, resisting the urge to punch her in the face. How could she be so perky and cheery after an twelve-hour graveyard shift?

"There, I'm done poking you for now. We'll be changing shifts soon, so I needed to get your vitals for the next nurse."

I was about to ask if Kim would be my nurse again today, when Dr. Wheatherby walked through the door.

He smiled, "How are you feeling? Felt any signs of gas in your bowels, yet?"

"You'll be proud of me. I've been farting like crazy."

"I can confirm her statement," Chuck piped in.

"Great! Let me take a listen." He placed the stethoscope on my stomach. "It does sound like things are starting to wake up. Excellent."

"Can I get the catheter out today?"

"I think it can be arranged."

"Oh, thank God. You don't know how much I hate having this in."

"I know, but it's better to keep it in if you need it rather than having to put it back in again. There's a higher risk of infection."

"I understand but thank you."

"No problem. Okay, I'll check back in on you later," he said, vanishing through the door.

"Awesome! If I can get this catheter out today maybe I can go home tomorrow. Hey, do you think we could visit David this morning? I'm anxious to see him."

"I don't see why not. Let me go home first, and when I get back, we can go."

"Perfect. Get going, then."

A few hours later, Mom arrived with Pops. Excited that someone had arrived who could help me, I enlisted her help to get me out of bed.

Mom pushed the button to lower my bed. Leaning on my elbow to balance myself, I inched my body closer to the side and then swung my legs around so they hung off the bed and my toes touched the white floor. Getting out of bed was still far more difficult and painful then I had expected.

How was David doing? I'd been told he had color in his cheeks and was asking for hamburgers, but I needed to see him for myself.

Mom helped me stand and walk the few short steps to the sink. My face fell as I glanced at the image in the mirror. A few weeks before the surgery, I'd cut my hair into a shoulder-length bob. Now, I regretted the decision. It would've been much easier just to throw it up into a ponytail.

The only thing I could do with this tangled mess was pat it down with water and hope for the best. It didn't matter how I looked, though. I would see David soon—alive and well.

Chuck returned before lunch, and as promised, we headed for David's room. The hallway stretched on forever, as I anticipated our reunion. The last time I saw him, in the pre-op room, we were both nervous, not sure of what to expect but confident we would see each other again.

It felt surreal, all the work, the prayers, the endless

conversations with family, friends, doctors; all the testing—it was all coming together at this one moment in time.

Would he survive? Would he lead a normal life? What would he look like? Would he be in pain? What if something happened and his body rejected the kidney? How would I feel if it failed? Would all of this be for nothing? Would he hate me? How is his wife? His girls?

Paralyzed by the questions flying through my mind, I forced myself to breathe. Everything will be okay; I reminded myself.

Leaning against the wall outside David's door, I closed my eyes and prayed, *"Papa, I need you. I need you to help me walk through this door. Whatever happens, I thank you for allowing me to be a part of this incredible journey. Not only did you save David's life but I found You again in the process. I'm forever grateful."*

I felt Chuck grasp my elbow as he guided me through the door, giving me the strength to move forward. I entered David's room, and as my trembling hands covered my lips, tears spilled down my cheeks. My breath caught as I saw him for the first time since the surgery. Before me—a miracle. David was alive.

Our eyes locked, and he motioned for me to come closer. Taking my hand in his, he whispered, "My Amy-Angel. Thank you!"

I swallowed hard before answering, "You bet. Anytime."

CHAPTER THIRTY-ONE

"My grace is all you need. My power works best in weakness." —2 Corinthians 12:9

BACK IN MY ROOM, I laid my head on the pillow as memories of the day's events swirled in my mind. The difference in David's appearance from only a few days before was astonishing. His once almost lifeless body had a healthy, pink vibrancy, and the twinkle in his eyes made me smile.

I hadn't expected such a rapid change. I knew donating my kidney was the right decision. Even the physical changes in his wife, Suzanne, were fantastic to witness. Just days before, her face had held years of worry and anguish. Her eyes, once hollow and hopeless now shone with joy and life.

Earlier, I'd gone for my afternoon walk, when I heard, "Get out of my way. I can run!" Emotion leapt from my heart as I watched David zigzag down the hall holding an IV pole.

The doctors told me the surgery was harder on the donor than the recipient, but I didn't believe it until then. David had been in so much pain for the last couple of years. But now with his new kidney, he was pain-free and running.

For the recipient who was used to living in pain, receiving a life-saving kidney was like getting a jolt of electricity—everything suddenly felt good. But for a healthy donor, the effects of surgery were hard on the body. They weren't used to pain like the recipient.

Earlier, the nurses removed my catheter—one more step toward going home, I thought. The plan was for me to leave within the next day or two.

As daylight faded through the blinds, I smiled at Chuck and then drifted off to sleep.

I wasn't sure how long I'd slept, when I woke with a ball of pain in my stomach. Trying to catch my breath, I screamed, "Chuck, something's wrong. Chuck! Chuck!"

Chuck looked at me, wide-eyed and stunned. "What's wrong? What's wrong?"

"Get the nurse. The pain...get the nurse!"

Chuck sounded the emergency button on the remote. "It's going to be okay. The nurse is on her way."

"It feels like my bladder is going to explode." I doubled over as pain ripped through my abdomen. I hadn't been able to pee all day—nothing worked. I didn't tell anyone because I knew they'd put another catheter in and then I couldn't go home. I hadn't expected to hurt as bad as I did.

A thin, wiry nurse raced into the room, "What's wrong?"

"She's in pain and hasn't been able to go to the bathroom since they took the catheter out. Do something!"

The nurse felt my stomach and said, "Amy, your bladder is extended. I'm going to have to put in a catheter. You'll feel better in just a moment."

"No," I shrieked, "They won't let me go home... they won't let me go."

"It'll be okay, Amy. I need you to calm down." She paged for another nurse, and a large man with dark skin rushed into the room.

Oh, no—not a man! Could this get any more embarrassing? I felt sweat gathering at my hairline and a warm scream filled my throat as I felt a tube inserted inside me. Immediately, my body relaxed—the pain was gone.

"Well, it appears you had a full bladder, Miss Amy," the nurse replied. "You've already filled 500cc in just a matter of minutes. No wonder you were in such pain. Why didn't you tell us earlier?"

"I wanted to go home tomorrow." My words hung in the air as large tears formed in my eyes.

The nurse in sympathetic voice said, "Let's see how you're doing in the morning. In the meantime, try to get some sleep."

163

I shook my head.

Chuck brushed a piece of hair out of my eyes. "You gave me quite a scare tonight."

"I know. I'm sorry," I wrestled with feelings of defeat. My body had betrayed me, yet again, and I felt powerless to do anything about it.

"Close your eyes. I'm right here." Chuck's finger looped around mine. I felt my defenses melt away and once again, I slipped off into the darkness and dreams.

Early the next morning, I heard a muffled voice, "We're going to start her on a round of antibiotics. She can go home tomorrow, but she'll need to keep the catheter in until she sees the urologist."

"What? I can still go home?" I asked, trying to understand what I just overheard.

"Look who's awake. I heard you had an eventful night."

"Yes, but did you just say I could go home tomorrow? I thought I couldn't as long as I had a catheter?"

"As I was just explaining to your husband, in a perfect world, we would prefer you not have a catheter when we send you home. But your bladder hasn't started working yet, which is concerning. We are putting you on a heavy round of antibiotics to help with any infections and then you'll follow up with a urologist this week."

"But I can go home?"

"Yes, you can go home tomorrow."

"Thank you!" I replied.

The day seemed to drag on forever. I made my usual walk to the nurse's station and back. I finally got the damn ball to reach the black line on the breathing torture chamber, and David was released.

The doctors explained sometimes the recipient would leave before the donor. I didn't think it would be the case for us because I was young and healthy but, in fact, David had left this morning.

Chuck told me before David left, he had gone to ring the chimes in honor of his donor. This was a special tribute to donors, and only recipients were allowed to ring the chimes on the day they were released from the hospital. It wasn't often the joyful sound filled the hall, so today was a special day. David went home alive—a miracle.

"It'll be okay," Chuck said in a reassuring tone.

"Was I naïve to think I would be immune to side effects from the surgery?"

Chuck leaned over and kissed me full on the lips and, with his voice as soft as butter said, "I love you, Amy. You're my world."

CHAPTER THIRTY-TWO

"I am with you and will watch over you wherever you go."—Genesis 28:15

THE DOOR YAWNED OPENED, AND light from the hallway streamed in. A nurse, with a short boyish haircut, entered my room, "I'm sorry. I didn't mean to wake you."

"Have you seen Dr. Wheatherby, yet?"

Just then her shadow was joined with another and Dr. Wheatherby replied, "Did I hear my name? Is someone ready to go home?"

"When can I leave?" I felt like a kid on Christmas morning. Everyone at the hospital had been great, but I was beyond ready to leave.

"We've got some paperwork to do, but hopefully you'll be home by lunch time. How are you feeling?"

"Tired but good. I couldn't sleep—too excited."

"Hopefully, you'll sleep better tonight. I've made you an appointment with Dr. Darzi, a urologist, for tomorrow. Make sure you keep it. Also, I'm giving you a prescription for antibiotics and pain medication. And Dr. Peterson will see you in two weeks for a follow-up. Any questions?"

"Nope. Chuck, do you have any?" I asked him.

"When will she get the catheter out?" Chuck asked.

"Dr. Darzi will determine it tomorrow. He'll probably give it a few more days for the antibiotics to work."

"Great! Thank you, for everything." Chuck grabbed the doctor's hand and pumped it. A pleasant aroma of bacon and eggs wafted in from the hallway.

"Looks like breakfast has arrived. I'll leave you both to eat. Call me if you need anything; otherwise, I'll see you in two weeks."

Dr. Wheatherby left as a locomotive of a woman with a broad, pulpy face came in carrying a breakfast tray.

"Good morning, Miss Amy. How are ya' doin'?" she asked depositing the tray on the table before me.

"Excellent! I'm going home today," I replied, almost dizzy with excitement.

"Well, 'um great. My name is Eleanor. Can I get you anything else?" Her aged-mottled hands lifted the covers from the plates.

I snatched a slice of bacon and broke it on my tongue—perfectly crisp and perfectly salty. The rich, bold scent of black coffee lingered in the air.

"Nope," I mumbled. "This is good. Thank you."

"You're welcome, ma'am. Good luck to ya'," Eleanor replied, waddling from the room.

"I must be hungry because these eggs are delicious." I dipped the buttered toast in the warm, gooey centers.

"I guess we should start packing. It looks like we're leaving."

"Yippeee!" I shrieked. "I feel like I've been in here forever. Can we pick up Maggie after we leave? Have you called to see how she's doing?" I missed my puppy.

"Yes, I called yesterday. Maggie's fine. I'll go get her tomorrow."

"But why aren't we getting her today?" I asked in an almost whiney voice. I terribly missed Maggie.

"I think we need one night at home to get you settled. She'll want to jump on you and be on your lap."

"She'll be okay," I protested.

"Let's see what time it is when they spring you and then we'll decide. Okay?"

"Sure. Whatever," I mumbled. I knew Chuck was trying to help, but I missed my "Moo." Just then, the nurse from earlier walked in, and thoughts of Maggie moved to the back of my mind.

"I need to remove your IV, so you can get dressed."

"Perfect, thank you," I replied. We chatted back and forth as the nurse unplugged the lines attached to the IV. I found out her name was Joyce, and she had been a nurse for about ten years.

"I'll be done in a minute. I'm just waiting on the discharge papers and then we can get you out of here."

"How long does it usually take?" I asked.

"A couple of hours."

I stared at the clock as if willing the hands to move. All my nervous glances and impatient shoveling of papers did nothing to make time move faster—it only succeeded in upsetting Chuck.

"Will you quit. The nurse will be in shortly. I promise."

"You said it a half hour ago. They're never going to let me go," I replied, with a long, dramatic pause.

"You're annoying. Why don't you call someone...your mother perhaps?"

I shrugged my shoulders. Mom would commiserate with me—Chuck clearly wasn't. I fished in my purse for my cell phone and glanced at the caller ID. There was a missed call from Mom earlier. Just as I began to punch her number on my phone, Joyce appeared in the doorway with paperwork in her hands. I snapped my phone down.

"Do you have the discharge papers?"

"Yes, Yes. Sit down so we can go over it."

I positioned myself on the edge of the lounge chair like a lioness ready to pounce on her carefully stalked prey. Glancing at me cautiously, Joyce reviewed the highlights of the discharge instructions.

Rest for the next two weeks. No heavy lifting. No showering or sex for two weeks to allow the incisions to heal—Chuck glared with disapproval. I can resume a regular diet. No driving until my follow-up appointment with Dr. Wheatherby.

If there were any problems, I was to go to the CMC Main emergency room, if at all possible, since the transplant clinic was there. I signed and initialed where instructed, stating I understood all directions regarding my discharge.

"Can I go now?" I asked, hardly suppressing a smile.

"As soon as someone from transport gets here with a wheelchair."

"I can walk," I demanded.

"It's hospital policy. They have to escort you to the lobby. Chuck, you can take her stuff to the car and pull it around, if you want. It shouldn't be much longer."

Within a few minutes, a tall man with black hair erupting in a curly, twisted tangle on the top of his head walked in with a wheelchair.

"Hallelujah! Let's go!" I shouted.

Charlie grabbed my elbow, as I stood up, and guided me into the wheelchair. "Let's go, Ma'am. Your chariot awaits."

"Thank you. Can you make this thing fly?"

"What's your hurry? Got someplace better to be?" He winked as he removed a Kleenex from his pocket to wipe off his glasses.

A girlish squeal escaped from my throat, "Yes, home."

"Well, then let's get going."

As Charlie pressed the elevator down button, I remembered my escort to the pre-op lobby, who had pushed the up button on the same elevator only a few days before. Unsure what was about to happen, his comforting presence calmed me as I walked through the hospital halls. Like, Charlie, he was a gift from God—angels escorting me to and from His miracle.

Would I have gone through with the surgery if I would have known how difficult the recovery would be? Yes, resounded in my head because God had used me as a conduit of His love.

We were greeted by a warm morning sun as we exited the hospital. Charlie locked my wheelchair in place. Closing my eyes, I baked in the sun's glow. Silently I prayed, "Thank You, Jesus, for touching my life in a way I never expected. You never leave me even when I leave You."

The words caught in the back of my mind, as I remembered the day Jesus saved my life.

I was five years old, and my mother had taken my brother and me to visit a friend of hers. An unusually hot day had prompted Mom's friend to invite us to swim at her neighborhood pool. My eyes went wide staring at the pool. Jamie, my brother, ran off with his buddy, leaving me to play alone.

Not knowing how to swim, I stood on the first step leading into the water, white-knuckling the railing beside me. I bit my lower lip as my eyes darted toward my mother, making sure she was still nearby.

At the opposite end of the pool, the older kids played a game of keep-away. Oh, how I wished I was brave enough to join them, but I stayed on the stairs watching from a distance.

Brittany, the daughter of my mother's friend, must have suspected what I was thinking because she drifted towards me with her hands on the bottom of the pool and her face just barely above the water. She looked beautiful and confident.

"Want to go over there?" she asked, nodding in the direction of the deep end. "I can take you if you want."

I spun around and yelled, "Mom, can I go with Brittany into the deep end? She said she would take me. Please, Mom! Please, can I go?"

"I don't think it's a good idea, Amy. Just stay on the stairs."

"But Mom!" I pleaded again.

"It's okay, Mrs. Gray. I know how to swim, and I won't take her far—just to the rope and back," Brittany responded.

Mom said, "Well, I guess it's okay but just to the rope and back. And Brittany, Amy doesn't know how to swim. So, be careful, please?"

Electricity shot off in all directions like fireworks within my tiny body. Mom said yes!

"I understand. I got her," Brittany replied and then swooped me up in her arms. As we moved closer to the rope which separated the babies from the grown kids, my heart raced like a running away train.

"Do you want to go under the rope? I can show you how to hold your breath for a few seconds."

My mind froze as I stared straight at her. Go under? Hold my breath?

"Come on," she giggled. "It's easy. Pinch your nose like this and take in a deep breath at the same time. You can also keep your eyes closed if you like."

I did as she said and pinched my nose with my thumb and index finger and then together we took in a deep breath. I closed my eyes and fixed my legs tight around her small waist. Instantly, we were underwater.

A few seconds later we resurfaced, and Jennifer exclaimed. "Wasn't it fun?"

I nodded with a shaky smile, wiping the water from my eyes with the back of my hands.

"We did it!" I shouted, when suddenly water drenched my

face again. A big blue ball landed with a loud thud right in front of us.

"Hey, throw it back," an older boy shouted. Brittany handed me the ball, and I chucked it in his direction. Excitement spilled out of me as if I'd gotten a large present on Christmas morning—I was part of the group.

We watched the older kids play awhile; then, Brittany's mom called her name and she dropped me.

I sank like a missile, and water rushed into my lungs. I tried grasping for Brittany—for anything which could help me. But my struggling went unnoticed. She was gone.

Wild with fear, I flailed my arms and legs frantically. My screams vibrated in my ears as darkness overtook me. I couldn't think of the word, but I knew I was drowning.

I stopped struggling. A golden white light resembling a giant hand—created a bubble around me. I could breathe. A voice whispered, "You're okay, Amy. I've got you."

As an adult looking back, I haven't the words to describe the unconditional love I felt in the bubble. Even the most exquisite words fall short. I know I was in the presence of the Divine Source.

I wanted to stay in the moment forever. Jesus understood and responded, "No, Amy, it's not your time. You have more to do but remember I AM always with you. I will never leave you. Now raise up your arm."

I didn't want to, but I raised my arm, and within moments someone pulled me out of the water.

Years later, I asked my mother how she found me. "I saw your arm sticking out of the water."

I could not have stood there by myself in the water with my arm raised because I couldn't touch the bottom. And I didn't know how to swim, much less tread water. Jesus saved me!

Did this experience transform me into the perfect angel? No, that wasn't how life would play out. It took me years to remember my moment with Jesus and what He told me. But He never left me—no matter how hard I fought to forget Him or God.

Arousing me from my thoughts came Chuck's voice as if an echo, "Are you ready to go home?"

Spots formed in front of my eyes as I blinked to open them. Above me, hawks circled lazily in the sky, an affirmation from the spirit world. Feeling the satisfying gleam of joy, I replied, "Yes. I'm ready."

CHAPTER THIRTY-THREE

"It is during our darkest moment that we must focus to see the light." —Aristotle

IMAGES FROM THE PAST WEEK unfolded in my mind as the TV blared in the background.

Content and happy to be home, I closed my eyes and drifted off to sleep. I don't know how many hours later it was, but I woke with a familiar pain in my abdomen.

"Chuck, something's wrong." I fumbled for the bag attached to my leg and held it up as proof. "I should have more pee, and my stomach hurts like it did in the hospital."

"I'm sure everything is fine. Let's give in another 30 minutes, and if it doesn't get any better, we'll call the doctor."

"No! You don't understand. We need to go to the hospital, now." Every muscle in my body tightened. I could feel something wasn't right.

We lived in Fort Mill just south of Charlotte, and it would've made sense to go to the hospital in Pineville, but the discharge nurse told us if there were any complications to go to the main hospital in uptown Charlotte—forty-five minutes away.

"Go faster!"

"I am, but I'm also trying to avoid the bumps in the road like you asked."

"My bladder is going to explode. Go faster."

A full moon lit up the sky illuminating the road. I thought how beautiful it looked but remembered my mother's comments about how a full moon brought out all the crazies to the hospital.

"Call David's brother, Randy. He's an air medic at the hospital, right? Maybe he's working, and if the emergency room is busy, he might be able to get me in quicker."

Chuck called, and thankfully, Randy was working and agreed to meet us.

Thank you, Papa, I muttered under my breath. Even though I was panicked, I also felt the Presence of God. This innate feeling reassured me I'd be okay. A peace I couldn't explain calmed me—until I walked in the E.R. and realized that the crazies had arrived in full-force.

People littered the room. A small crowd was parked in front of a long desk waiting to speak to a round, dumpling of a man. Gulping in a deep breath, I just knew my bladder would explode right here.

Randy, wearing a Med-Air suit, suddenly appeared through the sliding doors pushing an empty wheelchair.

"Amy, I have a room ready for you," he said, bypassing all the usual pleasantries. He nodded at Chuck with an unspoken male-speak.

A twinge of guilt surged through me as Randy pushed me passed the others waiting helplessly. Absently, I twirled my wedding ring pretending not to notice.

Chuck and Randy helped me onto a gurney in a small room just past the nurses' station. Outside, people bustled from one place to another, barking commands.

"This place is a madhouse tonight—full moon. A nurse will be in shortly to get your vitals and take down your information. Then, we'll move you to an examining room where you'll see a doctor," Randy explained.

"I don't think I can wait that long," holding up an almost empty catheter bag. "Something is wrong. My bladder is painfully full, and it feels like it's going to burst. Can it happen?"

"Let me see if I can get a nurse in here."

Randy left to talk with the nurse standing directly in front of us. I couldn't hear the conversation, but she nodded her head, closed the chart in her hands and headed in my direction.

"Hello, Amy. My name is Miranda. Randy tells me you donated a kidney to his brother a few days ago—it's an amazing thing to do."

"Thank you, but something's not right. Please help me."

Miranda grabbed the catheter bag and asked, "When did the pain start?"

"A few hours ago. I woke up with a searing pain in my stomach. There should be more urine in the bag."

"The catheter is probably blocked. We'll need to put in a new one. Let me see what I can do. Hold tight, okay?"

With nothing else to do, I stared at the ceiling, attempting to calm my nerves. I counted the stain-mottled tiles at least a hundred times before Miranda finally returned.

"I'm going to move you to an exam room now. There was an emergency which came in right before you, and all the doctors are busy. I'll get you comfortable until someone can see you."

Randy explained that until a doctor could perform a physical exam, they couldn't replace the catheter. We had to wait. And as we passed gurneys lining the hallway filled with people, I knew it would be a while. I willed my bladder to cooperate.

Once I was in the exam room, Miranda grabbed my wrist and silently counted my pulse. "On a scale of one-to-ten, how bad is the pain?"

"A twenty," I replied.

"Okay. I'm going to give you some pain medicine. It should make you more comfortable."

Chuck and Randy talked, attempting to fill the awkward

emptiness in the room. I laid there quietly, closing my eyes, begging my thoughts not to betray me but unfortunately, not winning the battle.

Miranda returned as promised with a needle. She grabbed my right arm and tapped the battered purple vein twice looking for even the smallest of entry. But I knew it was hopeless.

"I'm not sure you'll find a good vein—they are in terrible shape from the surgery especially in my right arm, but unfortunately, my left is not much better. Can't you just give me a pain pill?"

"This will help you faster. Let me try, okay?"

She untied the rubber band from my upper arm and moved it above my elbow. "There I have one."

I felt a pinch, and I turned my head away as the needle burned through my skin. She squeezed the contents into my forearm.

A scream echoed through the room as it tore through my throat. The medicine Miranda had administered exploded in my arm. Immediately, my skin swelled, and I yanked my arm away.

"What in the hell do you think you're doing? Stop!" I cried as an intense, brilliant, pain seared through my arm, "Don't touch me!" A gang of tears spilled from my eyes.

The color drained from Miranda's face as she stared wide-eyed. Her lips opened as if to say, "I'm sorry," but then they snapped shut. She swallowed hard, and with a barely audible voice she stammered, "Let me get someone else."

Randy fell in right behind her and said, "I'll be right back."

"Oh my God! I'm terrible. She was only trying to help me, but the pain is excruciating. I just reacted." My shoulders heaved with raw emotion, unwilling to back down as Chuck held me tight.

"Shhh—it's okay. Randy has gone to find another nurse. Let me see your arm."

I held it out for him to see. "Wow, I think it's going to leave a mark! People are going to believe I beat you now," he said attempting to lighten the room with laughter.

I loved how he could always make me laugh. Punching him in the chest, I replied, "Stop! It hurts."

Randy returned, and as I presumed, with a new nurse. Slightly older than Miranda, I thought she might have more experience—I prayed anyway.

"This is Becky, and she's the ER nursing supervisor. If it's okay with you and Chuck, Becky and I are going to replace your catheter?" His eyes locked with Chuck's. "Chuck, it means... umm...do I have your permission?"

"Yes, of course. Do whatever you need to."

Randy grabbed the round, rolling stool, and Becky handed him two plastic gloves which he immediately snapped on. Folding up his sleeves he said, "Amy, I'm going to remove your current catheter and then I'll insert the new one. You should feel immediate relief."

I smiled in appreciation and laid my head back. What a night!

I never would've seen this coming. A few months ago, I didn't even know Randy, and now, we're getting more acquainted than I ever imagined, but I'm grateful God had him working tonight. I didn't know where I'd be without him.

As Randy and Becky replaced the catheter, my body melted into nothing. A resemblance of a smile formed on my lips as the extreme tension from only moments before faded away. The relief was incredible!

"Wow, I've never seen anything like this. You've filled almost the entire cath' bag in a matter of seconds. You must've been in pain," Becky exclaimed.

"Thank you," was all I managed to mutter. I closed my eyes and let my limbs fall loose. *Thank You, Papa!*

CHAPTER THIRTY-FOUR

"With God all things are possible." Matthew 19:26

STARING OUT THE WINDOW, I counted the street lights whizzing by—my mind dazed from the events of the night. My snapping at Miranda seemed a distant memory; however, I would've liked to apologize to her before I left. Randy said he would relay the message.

Staring at the moon, I noticed it had moved further into the darkness. Earlier, it shone bright and hung low on the horizon. But now, it looked like a small round speck far in the distance; yet, its immense power lit up the sky.

Grateful to be going home, I knew the grace of God had protected me from what could have been a horrific tonight. I relaxed into the moment, sucking in a deep meditative breath.

I could tell by his relaxed grip on the steering wheel that Chuck felt more at ease than he had earlier.

"What a night!" I said.

"Yes, but let's not do this again. Okay?"

"Agreed. Let me ask you, were you okay with Randy removing the catheter from my bladder? I saw the look between you two. The whole situation must've been uncomfortable. But I admit, even though I was embarrassed, I would've allowed the Pope to do it if I thought he could help."

"I was just grateful Randy was able to help. Now let's get you home and in bed."

I nodded as I shifted my weight in the seat, trying to get comfortable. I had to wear the catheter at least until I saw the doctor tomorrow but most likely for the rest of the week—it didn't make me happy. Having urine strapped to your leg wasn't sexy, but at least the catheter worked now.

Randy said scar tissue from the surgery somehow got into my bladder and clogged the tubing, keeping the catheter from working correctly. I learned tonight that bladders can and do explode, but thankfully, mine did not. Our bladder is a muscle which grows and constricts when needed, but it can also rupture if stretched too far—not a pleasant thought.

The next morning, I woke early as the pre-dawn light filled my room—creamy as lemon chiffon. The fluorescent numbers on my clock blinked 6:30. I had four hours until the appointment with the urologist, and after last night, I was looking forward to meeting him.

I found it ironic after donating a kidney, my bladder wouldn't wake up. Usually, I could pee on command. And now, I couldn't will myself to do it.

"Only temporary," I mumbled as I gingerly rolled to sit up. I dragged my feet off the bed in stealth mode, so I didn't wake Chuck up. But with my stomach still tender from the surgery and having the blasted urine bag attached to my leg, I didn't succeed.

"Do you need help?"

"No, no. Go back to sleep. I didn't mean to wake you. I'm fine." Chuck must have taken me at my word because a few moments later he fell back to sleep.

Slowly, I found my way downstairs. I hated to admit it, but I was glad Chuck suggested we'd wait to get my wonderful dog, Maggie, until after my doctor's appointment today. The house stood silent except for the rhythmic sound of heavy wheezing making its way from upstairs.

I don't know if it was being home or the intoxicating aroma of fresh, brewed coffee, but a feeling of contentment permeated my soul. Just then, I felt a familiar draft slide softly between my legs.

"Well, hey there, Suzi!" I winced bending over to gather up my silky bundle of kitty fur. She purred with contentment as I kissed the top of her head and nestled her under my chin. "Good morning, sweet thing. Want to sit on the couch with me?"

Suzi curled in beside me, and we watched the birds outside, dance from tree to tree through the patio window. Mesmerized by the fluidity of their motions, memories of the past filled my mind as if on a movie screen. I opened the pages of my journal and began to write.

Papa, thank you that Randy was available at the hospital last night. As busy as it was, his being there was a real miracle. He saved my life.

Thank you, also, that David is home and doing well. I ask You for a quick recovery for him.

"I can't believe all this has happened—its seems surreal.

"People continue to tell me I'm an angel and what I did was terrific. I've heard things like, 'I don't think I could have donated a kidney, especially to a stranger.' Or, 'you're such a good Christian to do something so selfless.'

What do I do with these comments? How do I respond?

Until I heard You tell me, I'd be the one, becoming a kidney donor was the farthest thing from my mind.

Why am I so uncomfortable with praise or affirmations? Maybe it's because part of me wants to indulge my ego and say, "Heck, yeah I'm an angel and what I did was wonderful and selfless. See how amazing I am?" But on a soul level, it's not why I'm here.

The struggle between my ego and my higher self is an illusion created entirely by my ego. Learning to let go and love myself unconditionally the way You love all Your creations has been an incredible journey, although, I don't know if I'm there, yet. Do we ever arrive at complete surrender and unconditional love?

As a teenager, I fought hard not to believe in You because I didn't think You loved me. If You did, then Your love should've protected me from being hurt—raped, beat-up, humiliated. I felt dead inside and lived in the shadows of my most significant fear—being unlovable!

One day, I don't know when it happened, hope entered my soul, and I started to believe there was more to me—more to life than I'd thought. I wanted Your help. I wanted what other people had. I asked You for it. You gave me a son.

I'd never known love as strong as what I felt for this child. It was as if my heart, like the Grinch, grew a hundred times its size in one breath. I wanted to be worthy of his love and being called Mom.

As life went on, I continued to ask You to reveal Yourself to me, and it wasn't easy. It felt like I was peeling an onion, one layer at a time. Under each new layer, a part of my true self revealed—the illusion of reality crumbling with each new lesson learned.

Early on this journey of life with You, I heard, "build transitional housing for battered woman in Charlotte." I had no idea how to go about doing it. But You provided everything—the people, the resources—all I needed. You even taught me how to write a 501c3 application to become a non-profit organization (and I received it on the first submission—amazing!).

The doors opened, and woman and children received housing and hope for better lives. Miracles happened daily, and Your grace filled my life.

I had attached myself to my achievements and believed I had done everything myself. I left the space of gratitude and peace that's only found within You. Eventually, Mending Hearts closed and the separation I felt increased. Once again, I found myself living in the shadow of my greatest fear—being unlovable.

Fast forward to New Year's Day, the year of the kidney donation, and in a state of desperation and loneliness, these words formed in my mind, "Do what you did before."

Intuitively, I picked up a pencil, blew off the dust on my journal and began talking to You again. My thoughts flowed easily as if we were two old friends chatting over a cup of coffee.

I surrendered and said, "Use me for Your purpose. Reveal Yourself to me." I heard "Trust me, Amy!"—oh, and by the way, I need you to give your kidney to David. What?? You do have a sense of humor!

I've come to realize the separation I felt throughout my life is hell on earth. In the Lord's Prayer, it states, "…on earth as it is in heaven." To me, this means complete union with You—heaven indeed exists everywhere because You exist in each of us—not outside of us. Heaven is not a place or a destination but an experience to be lived in the present.

So, now I sit here with my fur-baby cuddled beside me, my pencil in hand, and all I want to write is thank you. I am blessed.

CHAPTER THIRTY-FIVE

"Out of difficulties grow miracles."
—Jean de la Bruyere

THE DOCTOR'S WAITING ROOM HAD mahogany bookshelves along the wall with large, leather chairs and a comfy-looking, designer sofa. It reminded me more of a wealthy person's living room than a doctor's office.

The grandfather clock in the corner chimed, as the short-hand reached 11-o'clock. My appointment was at 10:30 but we had arrived fifteen minutes early. I could tell Chuck was getting impatient; every few minutes he would exhale deeply as he shifted in the now not-so-cozy chairs.

"I'm sure it won't be too much longer. Remember the office had to work me in," I said, trying to reassure him.

Chuck glanced up from his phone, "I know. I'm going outside to stretch my legs. Will you be okay for a few minutes?"

"Sure, but don't be too long."

I knew "stretch my legs" was code word for "I need a cigarette."

Snatching the *People* magazine off the end table, I absently flipped through the pages when a woman, built like one of the sofa cushions, yelled, "Amy Gray-Cunningham?"

"Yup, I'm Amy."

She escorted me into a small room and motioned for me to sit in an oversized, gray vinyl chair. She got my name and date of birth and then proceeded to ask me additional questions as her fingers pounded the keyboard.

Chuck tapped on the door and poked his head in, "Can I come in? I'm Amy's husband."

"Yes," she replied, "Let me find another chair."

The exam room wasn't much bigger than my bedroom closet, and the nurse, Jane, filled up most of the space. I questioned whether Chuck would fit.

He must've thought the same thing because he immediately said, "Oh, no. I'm okay standing. Don't let me interrupt."

Jane finished with her reporting and told us Dr. Darzi would be in to see us shortly and asked if she could get us anything.

"We're fine, but thank you," I replied, as she turned sideways to leave the room.

"You may be fine, but I hope this doctor doesn't take all day," groaned Chuck.

"I'm sure it won't take all day."

"Well, I'm hungry!"

"Then you should've eaten something before we left," I snapped.

Chuck shook his head but let my statement go as he hopped onto the exam bed. We sat for a long time as silence gathered in around us. A rap-tap-tap on the door caused me to jump.

"Hello, I'm Dr. Darzi. You must be Amy, and you must be Chuck." He extended a long, manicured hand in our direction. He wasn't as handsome as Dr. Peterson. His skin had a warm tea color as if he spent a great deal of time at the beach or on the lake.

"I'm sorry to keep you waiting. I hope it wasn't too long?"

"No, no, we're fine," I said feeling Chuck's eyes boring into the back of my head. "Thank you for seeing me on short notice."

"Not a problem. Hopefully, I can help you today."

"Me, too!"

Dr. Darzi proceeded to explain what we've already been told by other doctors, the anesthesia causes everything in our bodies to go to sleep and sometimes it's hard for parts to wake up, which was what happened to my bladder. However, he believed I would gain full control of my bladder.

"I see they have you on antibiotics. Let's keep you on those for the rest of the week, and I think you should keep the catheter in at least until Friday. By then you should be fine. Do you know how to remove the catheter yourself, Amy?"

My breathing stopped for a split second, and my mouth fell open.

"Wh-wha-what do you mean remove the catheter myself?" I stammered, thinking the information would've been useful last night.

"Oh, they are simple to put in and take out. People do it at home all the time. I'll have one of the nurses show you how to do it before you leave today."

"Okay," I replied dumbfounded.

"This is the plan. We're open on Friday until one o'clock. I want you to remove the catheter by 8 a.m., and if you haven't urinated by say around 11, then call the office, and we'll go from there. However, I'm not expecting any problems. I think your bladder just needed a few extra days," he said in a soothing tone with a gentle pat on my hand. "Sound like a plan?"

"Sure! I pray it's as simple."

"It will be. Now let me get one of the nurses, and we'll get you out of here."

"And the best news I've heard all day," Chuck beamed slapping his hands together.

"If everything goes well on Friday—which I'm confident it will, then I want to see you back in two weeks after you've finished the antibiotics."

"All-righty!" I wished I had his confidence. "See you in two weeks." And hopefully not sooner, I thought.

Dr. Darzi winked, shutting the door behind him.

CHAPTER THIRTY-SIX

"I believe that if one always looked at the skies, one would end up with wings." —Gustave Flaubert

THANKFULLY, THE NEXT FEW DAYS were uneventful. I rested which is probably what my body and mind needed to heal. Family and friends checked in with me periodically.

Tom Roussey with WBTV called. "I'd like to do a follow-up interview with you when you're up to it. I think your story is one of immense courage and faith, and viewers would like to know how you're doing."

"I'd love to, but can it wait until next week?"

"Yes, of course," Tom replied.

We set a date for the following week. Tom also planned to call David to see if he'd like to take part in the interview, as well.

I wondered how David was doing, and I made a mental note to call him later.

Pressing back tears, I thought of the little things God gives us to be grateful for—like merely breathing and opportunities to make a difference in the lives of others, no matter how big or small.

Curled on the couch with a steaming cup of coffee, I allowed my mind to quiet as the world dissolved in silence. I heard a faint voice, "Are you ready to remove the catheter?"

An enormous smile exploded on my face. Was I ready? Of course, but for a brief moment fear rose, and I questioned, "What if it doesn't work?"

Determined, I reeled in my thoughts and responded to Chuck, "Let's do it. No time like the present!"

In the downstairs bathroom, the silence between us stretched as tight as a bubble ready to pop. Chuck reached between my legs, "They said this shouldn't hurt but let me know if it does."

My eyes fixated on the picture hanging on the far wall as my face, neck, and ears felt impossibly hot. Since all this started, Chuck had gone above and beyond, and once again he was seeing more of me than he probably wanted to. Although embarrassed, I was grateful I could count on him.

"There—now go pee!" he said in a joking tone.

"I'm planning on it."

"Well, I'm going back to bed. It's way too early for me. Wake me up when something happens."

"I will, and Chuck...," I paused as our eyes lock, "Thank you! I couldn't have done this without you."

"I know!" He flashed a winning smile and headed upstairs. I settled in on the couch with water and coffee in both hands, willing my bladder to cooperate.

CHAPTER THIRTY-SEVEN

"Never will I leave you; never will I forsake you."
—Hebrews 13:5

STARTLED, I WOKE UP TO my iPhone buzzing—a text message from Mom. I'll call her later, I thought. My brain was still foggy from a crazy nightmare about an ex-boyfriend, Tom, who had introduced me to cocaine. Weird—I hadn't thought of him in years.

The memories of him and that period in my life were like reading a book where the characters were familiar but not necessarily real. It's hard for me to wrap my mind around the fact I was "that girl" who had participated in hurting so many people, including myself.

About a year after we broke up and I had gotten clean, I ran into Tom's parents at a restaurant where I waited tables. It was a hectic Saturday morning, and they were seated in my section.

Rushing by the table I announced, "I'll be right with you." Immediately, my body locked into place—almost dropping the coffee pot.

Tom's father peered over his glasses and shot me a look of what I could only assume was disgust and hatred. My heart skipped, and bile filled my throat.

I knew his parents blamed me for the trouble Tom found himself in with drugs and the police. I heard from my lawyers that he was still in Georgia and had several warrants for his arrest.

During their breakfast, his parents informed me Tom was engaged to a "nice" lady, was no longer doing drugs, and Tom and his fiancée were expecting a baby. Jealousy and guilt tugged at my heart. I wanted to be happy for him—truly, but I wasn't ready to let go of the hurt and resentment, yet.

By the grace of God, I survived the encounter with his parents and, thankfully, I had not run into them or Tom, again.

A smile formed on my face as I remembered the three pennies they left on the table. Those three pennies said a thousand words—loudly.

I still don't know how I was never arrested for the cashing of stolen checks and stealing a car. But, maybe jail wasn't supposed to be part of my life story.

With several felony warrants and the possibility of serious jail time looming over me, somehow my mom worked out a deal where I paid restitution and agreed to attend drug treatment. As a result, though, I had to drop out of high school to work full-time to pay off what I owed.

One of my biggest regrets in life was missing the experience of walking with my graduating class to receive a diploma. I did, however, earn a GED from a local community college and, eventually, an undergraduate degree from an online college.

I remembered when I started college, my dream was to participate in the graduation ceremony. I saw myself in a cap and gown walking across the stage with my family in the audience and reaching out to receive my diploma.

But as life would have it, the same weekend of my graduating ceremony, my son, Alex, graduated from high school. And, I wouldn't have been any place else, but with him.

Watching Alex grow into the beautiful man he had become was my greatest blessing. When he walked across the stage, in a way he not only did it for himself, but for me, too. We had grown up together, and I was eternally grateful he had chosen me to be his mom.

He forced me to take responsibility for my life and the choices I made. My life wasn't mine own anymore—I had someone who needed me.

I grabbed my journal and began writing;

Papa, I'm not sure why of all days I dreamed about Tom. I haven't thought of him or my life back then in years. Maybe it was to remind me of how far we've come. You can take even a lost drug addict and perform miracles. I thought kicking cocaine was a miracle, but it was in fact only the beginning.

I'm blessed to have been a part of something so great this past week. But, I know it's only one ripple in a large pond filled with ripples.

Thank you, Papa! Amen.

I laid my journal and pencil down and headed to the bathroom. Now was the time. I sat on the toilet and waited as a long, silent minute dragged past. I took in a deep, meditative breath and then I heard a soft tinkle hitting the water.

Tears poured down my face as gratitude and relief washed over me. Was this what David felt the first time he peed after getting a new kidney?

I flew up the stairs and bolted into our bedroom, screaming, "I peed! Chuuuuuck! Chuuuuck!"

"Awesome, honey. I'm happy for you," Chuck replied with one eye barely open.

"Chuck, did you hear me? I peed!" I said again a little disappointed by his lack of enthusiasm.

"Yes, honey. Congratulations. Now, can I go back to sleep?"

"Whatever!" I repeated as I headed back downstairs to call Mom. I knew she'd join in my excitement.

EPILOGUE

"The thing about growing up with Fred and George," said Ginny thoughtfully, "is that you sort of start thinking anything's possible if you've got enough nerve." — J.K. Rowling (Harry Potter and the Half-Blood Prince (Harry Potter, #6))

OTHER THAN AN UNRESPONSIVE BLADDER, I haven't experienced any side-effects from the kidney donation. My one kidney functions better than a person with two, and besides limiting anti-inflammatory medication, such as aspirin, Advil or Aleve, I'm not restricted to a particular diet or physical activity. (Our kidney's filter anti-inflammatories—interesting tidbit.)

After the surgery, I followed up with the Transplant Clinic, periodically, for two years and with each visit, my kidney function continued to increase. Now, my creatinine levels are checked yearly by my primary care doctor, and thankfully, for the last seven years, all the tests have come back above normal limits.

Thankfully, Chuck and I didn't experience any financial repercussions from my time out of work. After speaking with the financial advisor at the transplant clinic, we decided it was time to let my employer know about my plans to become a kidney donor.

I was surprised to find out that the short-term disability offered through my employer paid hundred-percent of my salary while I was out on leave for eight weeks. Typically, most short-term disability benefits will only cover sixty to seventy percent of an employee's salary. My employer, however, offered excellent benefits, and I was only required to take one week of paid vacation before the short-term disability benefit became effective. Another miracle from God!

Becoming a living kidney donor was not even a thought until I heard God tell me "I'd be the one." Heck, I didn't even know you could donate a body part while alive.

But my story is more than just about giving a kidney.

David, a man I didn't know, was dying and when I heard his story, I felt an intense desire to help him. In the beginning, I questioned my sanity, but at the same time, I had a feeling of peace within me which surpassed all understanding.

The turning point for me was when Jennifer, David's sister, told me we would declare the kidney donation into existence. I didn't understand her statement then, but looking back on it, I do, now.

We dared to believe what I heard was true. We saw the end result. We saw David as healthy, vibrant, and alive. Jennifer thought this miracle into existence when she created the Facebook page, and then showed me how to believe it, as well.

I'm not saying everyone needs to become a kidney donor. But what's your story? What are you pulled to do? What are your dreams?

If we can imagine it, we can create it.

God spoke the world into existence with His words. *"And God said…"* (Genesis 1:3) Just think—His imagination created the universe!

When I established Mending Hearts—transitional housing for battered woman and children—I had no idea at the time that the way to make it happen was to declare it into existence by my imagination through Spirit.

A group of us believed with all our hearts that every person is entitled to safe housing free from intimidation, violence, and fear. Although Mending Hearts eventually closed, transitional housing is no longer a need in the Charlotte area because other people carried on the same vision.

The Wright brothers imagined flying in the air like birds. Today, we have airplanes, jets, and helicopters. What would have happened if they hadn't dared to believe? What would've happened had they not entertained a crazy thought? Where would we—the collective universe—be?

Think about what could happen if we all truly believed anything was possible? Imagine the possibilities.

The Bible states;

"...with God, all things are possible." —Matthew 19:26

"Ask, and it will be given to you; seek and you will find; knock, and the door will be opened to you."—Matthew 7:7

But we have to believe and act as if what we ask for is real. We have to free ourselves from fear and doubts and allow God's Spirit to move through us—allowing the universe to give us our full desires.

If you are on dialysis and are in need of a kidney, or any organ transplant, dare to believe in your healing. I firmly believe, when we are healed others are healed, too. So, it's not selfish to desire physical healing or selfish to ask for what you want.

See your 1-in-20-million match in your mind's eye and see yourself healthy, alive, and vibrant the way Jennifer and I saw David. Allow this image to permeate every part of your being and your thoughts. Create a vision wall with pictures and quotes that reinforce your desires.

Then, dare to believe in the impossible and let go of all attachment to the outcome. Allow God—Source—the Universe—to bring you complete healing by whatever means necessary.

I recently heard of a radical idea where scientists were creating human organs with 3D printing and the DNA from the person needing the organ. Imagine the possibilities!

At one-time electricity was an extreme, insane concept and now we don't even think about it as we reach for the switch to turn on the lights.

Dare to believe—you'll never know what could happen.

Today, David is the proud grandfather of a beautiful little boy. His grandson's life is forever blessed because of the love of his Papaw. This was one of the many ripples in our pond.

David's youngest daughter, Leslie is engaged to marry her high school sweetheart, and by God's grace, David will walk her down the aisle just as he had with Mallory.

David, and his beautiful wife, Susanne, enjoy traveling the country, and since he's no longer reliant on dialysis, they can fulfill their dreams of vacationing in fascinating cities. My heart sings each time I see pictures of them on Facebook at the beach or in the mountains or just being with family. Simply, amazing!

As a result of my experience as a kidney donor, and subsequent author of this book, each morning when I wake I ask, *"How can I serve You today, Papa?"* and I wait for the doors to open. I believe in the power of thoughts which become words, which lead to actions, which form habits, which build character, which finally, become our destiny (Lao Tzu).

So, ask yourself, "How can I serve today?" and then wait in hopeful expectation for miracles.

What are you thinking right now? What will you dare to believe is possible.

About the Author

Amy Gray-Cunningham is an author, speaker, blogger and a living kidney donor. She's lived in Charlotte, NC for over 30-years where she met and eventually married her high school sweetheart, Chuck Cunningham on September 26, 2009. Together they have two (almost grown) sons – Alex, 23 and Chase, 22

Amy is available to speak at your place of worship or your next group meeting. She loves sharing her story about the miracles of God in her life. For more information, please visit www.amygraycunningham.com or email her at amygraycunningham@gmail.com

"Amy is truly an amazing person. Her story on being a living kidney donor is completely inspirational and provides true insight on how one selfless decision, by listening to your heart, can create a new life for someone on the verge of losing all hope." —Katey Cipriani, Program Manager, National Kidney Foundation.

Additional Resources

For more information about becoming a kidney donation visit the National Kidney Foundation at:
www.kidney.org/transplantation

Donate Life America
www.donatelife.net

Organ Procurement & Transplantation Network
optn.transplant.hrsa.gov
www.organdonor.gov

United Network for Organ Sharing
www.unos.org

Other National Kidney Foundation Programs

Have questions about kidney disease? We can help!
NKF Cares
https://www.kidney.org/nkfcares

Talk to someone who's been there!
Speak with a trained peer mentor who will offer support and share their experiences with you.
https://www.kidney.org/patients/peers

Made in the USA
Coppell, TX
12 September 2023

21542919R00132